D0072978

RISKY SEXUAL BEHAVIORS AMONG AFRICAN-AMERICANS

RISKY
SEXUAL BEHAVIORS
AMONG
AFRICAN-AMERICANS

Ernest H. Johnson

Westport, Connecticut
London

Library of Congress Cataloging-in-Publication Data

Johnson, Ernest H.
    Risky sexual behaviors among African-Americans / Ernest H.
  Johnson.
        p. cm.
    Includes bibliographical references and index.
    ISBN 0–275–94162–0 (alk. paper)
    1. AIDS (Disease)—United States—Risk factors.   2. Afro-Americans—
  Health and hygiene.   3. Afro-Americans—Sexual behavior.   4. AIDS
  (Disease)—United States—Epidemiology.   I. Title.
  RA644.A25J63   1993
  614.5'993—dc20   92–28483

British Library Cataloguing in Publication Data is available.

Library of Congress Catalog Card Number: 92–28483
ISBN: 0–275–94162–0

First published in 1993

Praeger Publishers, 88 Post Road West, Westport, Connecticut 06881
An imprint of Greenwood Publishing Group, Inc.

Printed in the United States of America

∞™

The paper used in this book complies with the
Permanent Paper Standard issued by the National
Information Standards Organization (Z39.48—1984).

10 9 8 7 6 5 4 3 2 1

In memory of my sister Danette
and her son Brandon

Contents

Tables and Figure

FIGURE

Acknowledgments

To my family and friends who provided support, many ideas, and lots of constructive criticism.

I am forever indebted to Mr. Douglas Gilbert for providing the statistical support for this project. Thanks for hanging in there, and for your willingness to go far beyond the call of duty over the last few years. Best wishes with your career in Behavioral Medicine/Health Psychology.

I would also like to acknowledge a truly gifted African-American graduate student who claims that I provided part of the foundation for her career plans. If anything, she provided much of the enthusiasm for me to go forth with this project. To Yvonne Hinkle, I wish the best.

To Darlene Parker. Without your help the project would not have been completed on time. Thank you for your generous assistance.

Finally, I would like to thank Magic Johnson for coming forth with his story about how he contracted the AIDS virus. Hopefully, our public health officials and health educators will use this opportunity to implement culturally sensitive prevention programs that convince African-American brothers and sisters to sleep with their raincoats on and to make decisions about sexual behaviors based on facts rather than raging hormones.

CHAPTER 1

Introduction

Since the turn of the century, the overall health of all Americans has improved substantially. Although advances in medical and scientific technology have improved the health status of the American people, there is a growing concern and recognition that African-Americans have not benefited equitably from the fruits of science. Most African-Americans suffer poorer health than the non-minority populations. They die in larger numbers and suffer more illnesses and incidence of disease than the nation as a whole. Whereas these facts are not "new news," it is apparent that most of the public and the scientific community are not fully aware of the full impact of these problems. For example, African-Americans represent an increasing proportion of the population in the United States. The 1980 Bureau of the Census report indicates that one out of five persons in the United States is a member of a minority group, and that African-Americans are the single largest minority group, constituting 11.5 percent of the country's total population. The number of African-Americans in 1980 was 26.5 million, an increase of approximately 17 percent over the 1970 census figures.

The health status of African-Americans and other ethnic minorities became a national priority with the enactment of Medicare and Medicaid in the 1960s. Unfortunately, the nation did not recognize its importance again until 1984, when Secretary of Health, Margaret H. Heckler, commissioned the Report of the Secretary's Task Force on African-American and Minority Health to investigate and document the health status of minority populations and recommend strategies to ameliorate any problems that were revealed. The Task Force spent a year uncovering a wealth of data and compiling statistics on the health status and access to health care of African-Americans and other ethnic minority groups (Asian American/Pacific Islanders,

Hispanics, and Native American Indians). It documented the severity of the problems and defined the disproportionately large and consistent rate of mortality experienced among these minority populations when compared to non-minorities as a unique "health gap." This gap persists despite the recent twenty-year trend for improved health indicators for the aggregate population.

According to most leading health indicators, the rate of morbidity and mortality for the United States has been reduced. However, an examination of the same indicators for minority populations shows less of a decrease, and in some instances the indicators move in the opposite direction, with the gap in health status becoming wider. African-Americans have a life expectancy of 69.6 years compared to 75.2 years for non-minorities—a gap of over five years. Diabetes is 33 percent more common among African-Americans than whites, and African-American women have 50 percent more diabetes, especially if they are obese. Recent data from the National Center for Health Statistics indicate that African-American women, and to some extent African-American men, have the highest overall age-adjusted prevalence of obesity. It is estimated that 48 percent of African-American women are overweight, compared to 26 percent of white women, 30 percent of African-American men, and 25 percent of white men. Overall, African-Americans die of homicide at twelve times the rate of whites, of heart disease at a rate 27 percent higher than whites and from hypertension at a rate 40 to 50 percent higher.

These statistics were reported by the Task Force in its 1985 study, and it was estimated that each year 60,000 minority Americans die prematurely, 60,000 more than would have died had their health status been the same as white Americans. Sixty thousand excess deaths per year can be conceived as being nothing less than the result of neglect of the poor health of minority Americans or the tendency to deny the full impact of these problems. When the Task Force report was published in 1985, Secretary Heckler said that about 80 percent of early deaths result from cancer, heart disease, stroke, alcohol and drug abuse, diabetes, infant mortality, accidents, and murder.

Since publication of the report, the acquired immune deficiency syndrome (AIDS) has spread rapidly among members of the African-American populations, particularly among women of childbearing age. As of July 1990, 260,000 cases of AIDS have been reported worldwide (World Health Organization—WHO—1990). Because of under-reporting, WHO estimates 800,000 cases of AIDS with 8 to 10 million people infected with the AIDS virus. Projections made by WHO indicate that some 15 to 20 million people may be infected by the year 2000. In the United States, 135,644 AIDS cases have been reported with an estimated 1 million infected (Center for Disease Control—CDC—1990a; 1990c). It has been widely recognized that the population groups most affected in the United States have been white male homosexuals/bisexuals and intravenous (IV) drug abusers. However, since the mid-1980s there has been a marked shift in the routes of transmission and the population groups that are at risk, such that proportionately homosexual men account for fewer cases (from 66 percent of AIDS cases in 1986 to 57 percent in 1988), whereas IV drug abusers are accounting for more cases (from 17 percent to 24 percent). Similarly, when AIDS first appeared, it was largely confined to large cities such as New York, Newark, Houston, San Francisco, Los Angeles, and Miami. Interestingly enough, the numbers of AIDS cases continue to be greater for these cities. However, the number of HIV-infected persons has greatly increased in smaller cities and rural areas across the United States and the world, and every projection indicates that the AIDS crisis will become much worse.

What is alarming about these figures is that African-Americans comprise 24 percent of AIDS cases in the United States, and in a larger percentage of these cases AIDS was contracted through heterosexual intercourse. The burden that this disease and its related medical, social, and economic complications will have on African-Americans is almost incalculable without the implementation of aggressive research activities to understand the sexual behaviors and attitudes of African-Americans. Without a thorough understanding of these factors, it will be virtually impossible to develop culturally sensitive prevention and intervention programs that are effective in reducing the spread of AIDS.

It has been the case in the American public that as long as the AIDS epidemic did not touch anyone close to you, then it has been relatively easy to put AIDS out of mind. Remember the old saying "Out of sight—out of mind." Well, it appears that as long as AIDS was perceived as someone else's problem or something that happened to ghetto dwellers, drug addicts, or gays, then middle- and upper-class folks and heterosexuals who limited themselves to straight sex had nothing to worry about. However, when Magic Johnson stepped forward and announced that he had the AIDS virus, he put the risk of heterosexual transmission squarely in a new ball game. In other words, Johnson's claim that he was exposed to the AIDS virus by heterosexual contact, rather than intravenous drug use or homosexual contact, highlighted some very important questions about the heterosexual transmission of the AIDS virus. Questions such as: How easy is it to get AIDS from straight sex? How fast can the virus spread? Is the man or woman at greater risk in vaginal sex? How dangerous is oral sex? Are African-American male heterosexuals more at risk for being exposed to HIV/AIDS than males in other ethnic groups? Is it risky to participate in sports or share athletic facilities with people who are infected with the virus? What are the rules for deciding whether people with HIV infection qualify for Social Security benefits? These benefits often enable people with HIV infection to qualify for Medicaid or Medicare and to purchase expensive drugs that are needed to treat their illnesses. Given the fact that most people infected with HIV will develop AIDS, it will be important to see whether the administration will develop rules allowing benefits to be received by persons disabled by AIDS virus infections even though they do not suffer from the full-blown effects of the disease.

The fact that a few studies suggest that it is easier for the AIDS virus to be transmitted from an infected man to an uninfected woman led to the skepticism surrounding the manner in which Magic Johnson contracted the AIDS virus. Nevertheless, his claim that he has never had a homosexual encounter or used IV drugs clearly indicates that people can get infected through heterosexual contact. While it is true that the majority of AIDS cases in the United States as of 1991 are related to homosexual contact (54 percent) and IV-drug use (25 percent), the opposite is true worldwide where approximately 75 percent of the people who have the AIDS virus were infected heterosexually.

So, while the Magic Johnson case goes against the "popular" belief that heterosexuals who practice safe-sex are at low risk for getting HIV/AIDS, the case has provided the spark and momentum for thinking about whether the HIV/AIDS epidemic among heterosexuals in the United States could ever get as bad as it is elsewhere in the world. The actual prevalence of HIV infection among heterosexuals is very difficult to estimate because studies aimed at establishing the prevalence of HIV infection in the United States have not been systematically conducted. Since IV-drug users have a tendency to be concentrated in urban areas, heterosexuals living in large cities like New York, Houston, and Miami are more likely to encounter partners who are, or who have had previous sexual contact with them.

PLAN OF THE BOOK

This book describes the interrelationships between knowledge about AIDS, attitudes and emotional reactions associated with the use of condoms, previous history of being treated for sexually transmitted diseases, drug usage, and other relevant factors associated with African-American males and females who engage in risky sexual behaviors. Another aim of the book is to describe how the above fac-

tors are differentially related to gender and the perceived susceptibility of being exposed to AIDS and testing positive for AIDS.

The information assembled in this book was obtained from 200
African-American males and 205 African-American females (average
age 22 years) attending college in the southern part of the United
States. The study was prompted by the fact that a relatively large
percentage of AIDS cases (21 percent) are found among young adults
(age 20–29) (Centers for Disease Control, 1988), while approximately
70 percent of the AIDS victims are under 39 years of age.

The major risk factors associated with the transmission of AIDS
include: number of sexual partners, specific sex practices engaged
in with sexual partners (e.g., unprotected anal intercourse, oral-genital
intercourse), history of certain sexually transmitted diseases, substance use history, and the failure to use condoms. While researchers
are in agreement as to the importance of these risk factors in the
transmission of HIV/AIDS, few attempts have been made to understand the attitudes and sociocultural factors that contribute to these
high-risk sexual behaviors among African-American groups. Most
investigators have attempted to understand the sexual behaviors
and attitudes of African-Americans by comparing them to whites or
other ethnic groups. The basic problem with this approach is that
significant differences between ethnic groups (e.g., knowledge about
the transmission of HIV/AIDS; the practice of oral-genital sex) are
not likely to be significantly related to risky sexual practices within
the African-American groups. I am not saying that it is not important
to study ethnic differences in sexual behaviors, because the determination of consistencies in attitudes and behaviors across ethnic
groups can help our public health investigators to develop large scale
mass-media programs to reach several different ethnic groups at a
lower cost. However, what are we to do if the behaviors and attitudes
associated with risky sexual practices are not uniform across the
different ethnic groups? How will we realistically use the momentum
stirred-up by the Magic Johnson case to reach African-Americans if
in fact we have little information about the lifestyle and sexual behaviors that promote the transmission of HIV/AIDS among young
African-American adults? Whereas I don't profess to have the com-
plete answers to these or other questions raised throughout this
book, I do believe that the answers will have a greater degree of
validity and sensitivity if they are derived from studies of the variability of sexual practices within African-American groups. Therefore, the purpose of this book is to provide a balanced view, supported
by empirical data, of whether factors such as having multiple sex
partners, drug use, and risky sexual practices are related to the

prevalence of sexually transmitted diseases (STDs) and HIV/AIDS among African-American young adults.

Each chapter will review the current research pertaining to the topics discussed within the chapter and use the data gathered from the sample of African-American subjects to address specific questions. The first chapter provides an introduction, rationale and overview of the study that this book is based on. Basic information about the prevalence of AIDS among various African-American populations is presented. The final parts of this chapter focus on the medical characteristics and diseases associated with AIDS.

Chapter 2 describes the design and methodology of the study. Information about the subjects, measures of sexual behaviors, drug use, attitudes about the use of condoms, knowledge about AIDS, and perceived susceptibility of being exposed to HIV/AIDS is provided.

Chapter 3 presents information concerning knowledge about the transmission of AIDS with the major focus being to determine whether knowledge about AIDS varies as a function of demographic factors such as gender, age, education level, and marital status. The chapter also focuses on questions about whether knowledge about the transmission of AIDS is related to risky sexual behaviors.

Chapter 4 describes the sexual attitudes and behaviors of African-American males and females who are currently involved with multiple sex partners. This chapter describes the prevalence and reasons for involvement with multiple sex partners. The accuracy of information about the transmission of AIDS, history of sexually transmitted diseases, condom use, and certain risky sexual behaviors (e.g., unprotected anal-genital intercourse) are also discussed. The final part of this chapter attempts to determine whether individuals with multiple partners perceive themselves to be at greater risk for AIDS compared to individuals with a single partner.

In Chapter 5 I describe the sexual attitudes and behaviors of individuals who have been previously treated for sexually transmitted diseases. Their attitudes about the use of condoms, knowledge about AIDS, and use of drugs is described.

Chapter 6 describes the characteristics of individuals who "always" use condoms with their partner(s). I compare the attitudes and behaviors of this group with groups of African-Americans who don't use condoms but who vary in their intentions to use them. These comparisons help to identify attitudes and behaviors that should be targeted to motivate African-Americans to use condoms as a means of protection against exposure to the AIDS virus. The final part of this chapter describes whether the angry and negative emotional reactions associated with the use of condoms contribute to risky sexual behaviors.

In Chapter 7 the relationships between drug use and sexual behaviors is explored for males and females. I also describe whether the use of drugs is associated with risk of exposure to AIDS and sexually transmitted diseases. The final part of this chapter describes the relationships between risky sexual behaviors and the beliefs that African-Americans have about their perceived susceptibility to AIDS. Here, data concerning the attitudes, sexual behaviors, and drug use of individuals who are characterized as being at extreme risk of being exposed to HIV/AIDS are presented.

Chapter 8 describes the characteristics of individuals, males and females, who engage in anal intercourse. I also present data that describes the perception of risk, attitudes about using condoms, and knowledge about the transmission of AIDS for males and females who engage in anal intercourse.

Chapter 9 describes the characteristics of individuals who have tested positive for AIDS. Data is also presented for determining whether sexually transmitted diseases are co-factors for AIDS among the sample of African-Americans. Finally, the last chapter (Epilogue) is used to summarize the major findings described throughout the book and to present suggestions for AIDS prevention activities for young African-American adults.

The questions raised here will be of interest to many different groups including AIDS and sex researchers, epidemiologists, health psychologists, behavioral medicine specialists, individuals working in the area of infectious disease, medical students and Ph.D. students in health psychology/behavioral medicine, and other social scientists and health care professionals.

EPIDEMIOLOGY OF AIDS

The representation of African-Americans among people with the human immunodeficiency virus (HIV) exceeds their proportion in the general population by a factor of 2.3 (Coates, 1990; Centers for Disease Control [hereafter cited as CDC], 1988; 1989). In other words, although African-Americans comprise approximately 12 percent of the U.S. population, they represent roughly 26 percent of all cases of AIDS. This has been true since the first cases of HIV were reported in 1981. Although bisexual and homosexual contact between men continues to remain the most common mode of transmission among all ethnic groups, the alarming increase in the rate of HIV among heterosexual males who do not identify themselves as "gay," and women, warrants serious attention. This fact is especially important in light of recent findings which indicate that approximately 50 percent of all male heterosexual cases are African-American (CDC, 1989).

Several studies of the association between IV drug use and the spread of HIV have shown that a larger proportion of males with AIDS were heterosexual IV drug abusers or had a female sex partner who was a IV drug abuser (Des Jarlis, Wish, Friedman, et al., 1987; Mays and Cochran, 1988; Brown and Primm, 1988; Primm, 1990; Turner, Miller, and Moses, 1989).

The recent figures indicate that among women, the number of diagnosed HIV-1 cases climbed by 45 percent in the past year, and the rate of HIV-1 seropositivity among young adults (18 to 35 years of age) is doubling each year (Chu, Buehler, and Berkelman, 1990; Guinan and Hardy, 1987). HIV and AIDS are among the ten leading causes of death in women of reproductive age, and the death rate for HIV/AIDS quadrupled between 1985 and 1988 (0.6 per 100,000 to 2.5 per 100,000) with the death rate for African-American women (10.3 per 100,000) being nine times the rate for white women (1.2 per 100,000). Whereas IV-drug usage and other "needle" sharing behaviors account for some of the increase, the largest proportion of HIV cases appear to be a result of either sexual intercourse without condoms outside of monogamous relationships or from sexual intercourse with individuals with a "high risk" or increased probability of having being exposed to HIV (Mays and Cochran, 1988; Coates, Stall and Kegeles, 1988; Coates, 1990). While only 12 percent of women diagnosed with AIDS in 1982 were likely to have been infected through heterosexual contact, this figure rose to 26 percent in 1986 (CDC, 1988a, 1988b; 1989a, 1989b). African-American and Hispanic women comprised 77 percent of all women infected through sexual activity and it was estimated that heterosexual transmission of AIDS would increase seven times by 1992 (CDC, 1989; Guinan and Hardy, 1987; Bakerman, McCray, Lumb, Jackson, and Whitley, 1987).

Table 1.1 shows the distribution of AIDS cases by age group, exposure category, and race/ethnicity, reported through January 1991 for the United States. As can be observed, 161,288 adults/adolescents and 2,841 pediatric cases (younger than 13 years old) have been reported. Among the adults, the major exposure category accounting for 59 percent of all cases is through male homosexual/bisexual contact. Exposure through IV-drug use accounts for 22 percent and heterosexual contact accounts for 5 percent of the adult cases. Although there are a number of important differences between the different ethnic groups with regard to the primary routes of exposure, the major differences are that a larger percentage of African-Americans are exposed through heterosexual contact (11 percent), and the percentage of African-Americans (39 percent) and Hispanics (40 percent) who are exposed through IV-drug use (female and heterosexual male contact) is substantially higher than all other ethnic groups. Among the 2,841 pediatric cases of AIDS, the great majority of children (84 percent) were exposed through their mothers who have AIDS. The primary route by which these mothers acquired AIDS was through the use of IV drugs or having sex with an IV drug user who has been exposed to HIV/AIDS.

Table 1.2 shows the distribution of adult/adolescent AIDS cases by sex and exposure category for African-Americans reported through January 1991. A comparison of the data for males and females clearly reveals that a substantially larger percentage of African-American females than males were exposed through heterosexual contact (32 percent vs. 7 percent). As far as heterosexual exposure goes, the majority of cases occurred as a result of individuals having sex with IV-drug users. Among African-American males, the major exposure category was homosexual/bisexual contact which accounted for 44 percent of the cases. A relatively large percentage of males (44 percent) and females (57 percent) were also exposed through IV drug use. As indicated above, a larger percentage of African-American females than males are exposed to AIDS through heterosexual contact. It should be noted that in the areas of central Africa where HIV infection is extremely high, the great majority of persons exposed to the virus and who develop AIDS are heterosexual and the majority of the people do not have a history of homosexual activity, drug use, or blood transfusion (Clumeck, Sonnet, Taelman, Mascart-Lemone, DeBruyere, Van de Perre, Dashnoy, Marcelis, Lamy, Jonas, Eycksmans, Noel, Vanhaverbeek, and Butzler, 1984; Clumeck, Van de Perre, Carael, Rouvroy, and Nzaramba, 1985; Van de Perre, Rouvroy, Lepage, Bogaerts, Kestelyn, Kayihigi, Hekker, Butzler, and Clumeck, 1984).

In crowded African urban areas, the AIDS virus has become ubiquitous, threatening to kill off an entire generation of young men and women as it has done for some villages. According to figures released by the World Health Organization in the early 1990s, 75 percent of the people who have the AIDS virus throughout the world were infected through heterosexual contact. For example, in Africa, where one-tenth of the world's population accounts for half the estimated 10 million AIDS infections around the world, heterosexual transmission is the cause of at least eight out of ten cases. The same is true for Southern and Southeast Asia, where the epidemic is growing more rapidly than anywhere else on the globe. Among the prostitutes in Bombay's "red-light" district, 25 to 30 percent are HIV positive. HIV infection rates among prostitutes in Nairobi, Kenya are estimated to be higher than 90 percent. These high prevalence figures for the heterosexual AIDS transmission in Africa have been attributed to widespread venereal diseases such as syphilis and chancroid. The

Table 1.1
AIDS Cases by Age Group, Exposure Category, and Race/Ethnicity, Reported through January 1991, United States

Adult/Adolescent Exposure Category	White, not Hispanic No. (%)	Black, not Hispanic No. (%)	Hispanic No. (%)	Asian/Pacific Islander No. (%)	American Indian/Alaskan Native No. (%)	Total No. (%)
Male homosexual/bisexual contact	68,126 (76)	16,256 (36)	10,231 (40)	744 (75)	126 (54)	95,687 (59)
Intravenous (IV) drug use (female and heterosexual male)	7,139 (8)	17,654 (39)	10,271 (40)	44 (4)	38 (16)	35,229 (22)
Male homosexual/bisexual contact and IV drug use	6,212 (7)	2,896 (6)	1,548 (6)	21 (2)	32 (14)	10,726 (7)
Hemophilia/coagulation disorder	1,171 (1)	99 (0)	112 (0)	17 (2)	8 (3)	1,411 (1)
Heterosexual contact	1,854 (2)	5,157 (11)	1,578 (6)	37 (4)	10 (4)	8,656 (5)
Sex with IV drug user	1,003	2,322	1,221	16	7	4,581
Sex with bisexual male	281	159	59	9	1	510
Sex with person with hemophilia	71	7	3	1	—	82
Born in Pattern-II country	7	2,032	16	4	—	2,063
Sex with person born in Pattern-II country	42	85	8	—	—	136
Sex with transfusion recipient with HIV infection	105	27	27	1	—	162
Sex with HIV-infected person, risk not specified	345	525	244	6	2	1,122
Receipt of blood transfusion blood components, or tissue	2,618 (3)	648 (1)	394 (2)	71 (7)	6 (3)	3,737 (2)
Other/undetermined	2,135 (2)	2,263 (5)	1,368 (5)	64 (6)	12 (5)	5,842 (4)
Adult/adolescent subtotal	89,255 (100)	44,973 (100)	25,830 (100)	998 (100)	232 (100)	161,288 (100)

Pediatric (less than 13 years old) Exposure Category	White, not Hispanic No. (%)	Black, not Hispanic No. (%)	Hispanic No. (%)	Asian/Pacific Islander No. (%)	American Indian/Alaskan Native No. (%)	Total No. (%)
Hemophilia/coagulation disorder	96 (16)	19 (1)	23 (3)	3 (25)	—	141 (5)
Mother with/at risk for HIV infection	373 (61)	1,357 (92)	626 (86)	4 (33)	6 (86)	2,374 (84)
IV drug use	183	674	321	1	2	1,185
Sex with IV drug user	79	213	198	1	1	493
Sex with bisexual male	18	21	10	—	—	49
Sex with person with hemophilia	7	2	1	—	—	10
Born in Pattern-II country	2	212	3	—	—	217
Sex with person born in Pattern-II country	—	11	—	—	—	12
Sex with transfusion recipient with HIV infection	5	3	3	—	—	12
Sex with HIV-infected person, risk not specified	20	47	29	1	1	99
Receipt of blood transfusion, blood components, or tissue	17	19	12	—	—	48
Has HIV infection, risk not specified	42	155	49	1	2	249
Receipt of blood transfusion, blood components, or tissue	135 (22)	56 (4)	58 (8)	5 (42)	—	254 (9)
Undetermined	9 (1)	42 (3)	20 (3)	—	1 (14)	72 (3)
Pediatric subtotal	613 (100)	1,474 (100)	727 (100)	12 (100)	7 (100)	2,841 (100)
Total	89,868	46,447	26,172	1,010	239	164,129

Table 1.2
African-American Adult/Adolescent AIDS Cases by Sex and Exposure Category Reported through January 1991, United States

Male, Black, not Hispanic	Number	Percentage
Male homosexual/bisexual contact	16256	44
Intravenous (IV) drug use (heterosexual)	12959	35
Male homosexual/bisexual contact and IV drug use	2896	8
Hemophilia/coagulation disorder	93	0
Heterosexual contact	2488	7
Sex with IV drug user	729	
Sex with person with hemophilia	—	
Born in Pattern-II country	1479	
Sex with person born in Pattern-II country	38	
Sex with transfusion recipient with HIV infection	14	
Sex with HIV-infected person, risk not specified	228	
Receipt of blood transfusion, blood components, or tissue	348	1
Other/undetermined	1670	5
Male subtotal	36710	100

Female, Black, not Hispanic	Number	Percentage
IV drug use	4695	57
Hemophilia/coagulation disorder	6	0
Heterosexual contact	2669	32
Sex with IV drug user	1593	
Sex with bisexual male	159	
Sex with person with hemophilia	7	
Born in Pattern-II country	553	
Sex with person born in Pattern-II country	47	
Sex with transfusion recipient with HIV infection	13	
Sex with HIV-infected person, risk not specified	297	
Receipt of blood transfusion, blood components, or tissue	300	4
Other/undetermined	593	7
Female subtotal	8263	100
Total	44973	

reason for this is that these sexually transmitted diseases cause sores and infections that make it easier for the virus to pass from one person to another—a problem that is made worse by an inadequate medical system.

While few experts believe that what is going on in Africa or Southeast Asia will happen in the United States, the data presented in Table 1.2 shows that 32 percent of female and 7 percent of male AIDS cases among African-Americans reported through January 1991 were caused by heterosexual contact. One of the reasons for this may very well be that the prevalence of certain venereal diseases that make it easier for the virus to be transmitted through heterosexual intercourse are increased to almost epidemic levels among African-Americans. For example, although African-Americans make up approximately 12 percent of the U.S. population, they accounted for 76 percent of the syphilis cases and 78 percent of the gonorrhea cases (CDC, 1991a; Moran, Aral, Jenkins, Peterman, and Alexander, 1988).

So, while it may be true that the general level of hygiene and availability of treatment for STDs makes it unlikely that an African-style or Asian-style epidemic could sweep across the United States, AIDS is already epidemic among African-Americans and Hispanics in the poorest neighborhoods of Miami, New York City, Newark, Baltimore, and Washington. In addition to the rise in STDs in the inner city, mini-epidemics are beginning to appear in rural areas and small cities in parts of Texas and Georgia. As indicated earlier, a major reason why most experts believe that the United States is not likely to have an AIDS epidemic like Africa or Asia is the availability of treatment for STDs and the general level of hygiene. However, it should be pointed out that the AIDS epidemic in not static and that it is a dynamic problem that has hit the United States in three waves. The first occurred among homosexual men and the prevalence and incidence rates among this group are leveling off. The second wave involved IV-drug users who pass the virus in contaminated needles. The third wave, which involves a larger segment of the U.S. population, is just getting underway among heterosexual men and women who have "straight" sex with individuals in high-risk groups (e.g., IV-drug users, bisexuals).

According to the latest figures from the Centers for Disease Control, the risk to most heterosexuals in the United States is small, but it is growing steadily. Approximately 11,000 reported AIDS cases (6 percent of the 200,000 Americans affected over the past ten years) are related to heterosexual contact. While the percentage of AIDS cases attributable to heterosexual contact is relatively small (6 percent), it jumped to 40 percent during 1990 and it appears that the percentage is growing faster than any other group. In the United States as many as 1 million individuals may be infected with the virus that causes AIDS, but it is uncertain how many of the individuals were infected through heterosexual contact. In general, the great majority of AIDS cases (46 percent) reported through January 1991 were diagnosed when individuals were between 25 to 30 years old and 5 percent were diagnosed when individuals were less than 24 years old. The overall pattern of these observations tends to be consistent for males and females as well as for members of the different ethnic groups. There are a number of case studies which show that HIV transmission occurs between heterosexual persons (Calabrese and Gopalakrishna, 1986; Fischl, Dickinson, Scott, Klimas, Fletcher, and Parks, 1987; *Journal of the American Medical Association*, 1987a, 1987b; Redfield, Markman, Salahuddin, Wright, Sarngadharan, and Gallo, 1987) who have had no sexual contact with risk group members, but their sexual partner did. The study reported by Redfield et al. (1987) is particularly important because it studied male and female patients who acquired HIV through sexual contact with persons of the opposite sex. While several of the sexual partners were IV-drug users, the majority of the patients reported having a larger number of different heterosexual partners over the preceding 5-year period. Furthermore, most of the sexual contacts linked the HIV exposure to the partners who participated in unprotected vaginal intercourse.

Since its "discovery," AIDS has quickly become one of the most deadly diseases in history. Much like cancer, AIDS involves the immune system. It is caused by infection with human immunodefiency virus (HIV) and has a number of immunologic effects, including reduced responsiveness of lymphocytes to antigens, decreases in T-lymphocytes, some types of immunoglobins and T-helper lymphocytes. Because the virus attacks helper cells specifically, it disrupts cellular immunity and increases susceptibility to opportunistic infections. Thus many of the patients with AIDS develop other illnesses such as pneumocystis carinii pneumonia and Kaposi's sarcoma, which may actually be the cause of their death.

It is now recognized that exposure to HIV is not the same as having AIDS. However, once exposed an individual may develop the disease or a related syndrome which is referred to as AIDS-related complex (ARC). This syndrome is viewed as an intermediate stage in which symptoms are present and immunosuppression is detectable, but the intensity of the illness is more moderate. Nevertheless, in some cases ARC may be fatal and it appears to precede AIDS in most cases. For some individuals exposed to AIDS there may be no immediate symptoms, while less than half of those individuals who tested positive for AIDS (i.e., having antibodies for HIV) have developed AIDS. The virus appears to remain dormant for varying periods before becoming active and causing AIDS or ARC.

Although a number of treatments have been proposed and promising drugs have been developed, there is currently no cure for AIDS or vaccine to prevent infection by HIV. Because of this, prevention is particularly important, as once an individual develops the disease, the prognosis is not good. It is widely believed that the spread of AIDS can be greatly reduced or stopped by getting people to adopt safer sexual behaviors so as to minimize risk of exposure. The use of condoms during sexual intercourse, for example, greatly reduces the chances of spreading AIDS and STDs. It is also widely believed that certain behavioral (e.g., excessive drinking, use of illicit drugs, poor physical fitness) and psychosocial factors (e.g., high levels of depression and loneliness) may be co-factors that facilitate the progression from HIV to AIDS.

MEDICAL CHARACTERISTICS OF AIDS

AIDS is usually defined as an opportunistic disease or infection that is predictive of cellular immune deficiency and occurs in a person with no known preexisting illnesses or therapies that would produce immunosuppression. As can be observed, this definition of AIDS contains three components: (1) identification of an opportunistic disease; (2) establishment of cellular immune deficiency, either by clinical laboratory tests or by the presence of a disease associated with immunosuppression; and (3) ruling out alternative factors that might cause immune deficiency, such as lymphoma, leukemia, congenital immunodeficiency, or a history of steroid or other immunosuppressive therapies.

Research from independent investigators in France and the United States were the first to identify the unusual serum antibodies in AIDS patients. The virus responsible for the antibodies was eventually termed the human immunodeficiency virus (HIV). This retrovirus infects and attacks helper T lymphocytes, the cells that activate immune system functioning. Whereas the HIV antibody is commonly found in patients with AIDS, HIV antibodies are also present in patients who show some clinical symptoms of immune suppression but who do not have the clear-cut opportunistic infections characteristic of AIDS. For example, patients with persistent generalized lymphadenopathy, chronic enlargement of lymph nodes in multiple body sites unrelated to identifiable illness or infection and indicative of abnormal immune function, are also HIV antibody-positive 77 to 100 percent of the time (Bayer, Bienzle, Schneider, and Hunsmann, 1984;

Lang et al., 1987). Furthermore, depending on the geographical area and the behavioral characteristics of subjects recruited for research participation, HIV-antibody-positive rates among sexually active (but apparently healthy) homosexual males range from 20 to 60 percent (Anderson and Levy, 1985; Lang, Anderson, Perkins, Gant, Winkelstein, Royce, and Levy, 1987; Jaffe, Darrow, Echenberg, O'Malley, Getchell, Kalyanaram, Byers, Drennan, Braff, Curran, and Francis, 1985; Carlson, Bryant, Hinrichs, Yamamoto, Levy, Yee, Higgins, Levine, Holland, Gardner, and Pedersen, 1985). Other groups such as IV-drug users, hemophiliacs, heterosexual partners of persons with known HIV infection, and female prostitutes also exhibit higher than expected HIV seropositivity (Carlson et al., 1985; Redfield, Markman, Salahuddin, Wright, Sarngadharan, and Gallo, 1987).

It was estimated that by 1991 from 50 to 100 million people worldwide would have been exposed to HIV and antibody-positive (or seropositive). While the proportion of persons who are actively carrying the virus is not conclusively known, most HIV seropositive individuals are presumed to be infected (Melbye, Biggar, Ebbesen, Sarngadharan, Weiss, Gallo, and Blattner, 1984; Goedert, Sarngadharan, Biggar, Weiss, Winn, Grossman, Greene, Bodner, Mann, Strong, Gallo, and Blattner, 1984).

Persons with HIV antibodies are generally presumed to be carriers and, therefore, capable of transmitting the virus to others even when they show no evidence of illness. In fact, the majority of persons who are currently antibody-positive to HIV are asymptomatic and show no detectable clinical evidence of either immune suppression or illness. Nevertheless, no definitive conclusions about the health course of people who become infected by HIV can be offered except that a large proportion will eventually develop AIDS. The major reason for this difficulty is the long incubation period of the virus which ranges from 1 to as many as 14 years from initial exposure to clinical disease onset (Groopman, 1985; Peterman, Jaffe, Feorino, Getchell, Warfield, Haverkos, Stoneburner, and Curran, 1985; Seale, 1985).

The overall pattern of findings from the current research suggests that from 5 to 20 percent of persons infected with HIV will succumb to the disease within five years of infection (Curran, 1985; Francis and Petriccian, 1985; Groopman, 1985; Hessol, Rutherford, O'Malley, Doll, Darrow, and Jaffe, 1987). As indicated earlier, the length of the incubation period is believed to also be influenced by lifestyle factors or co-factors that may facilitate the spread and progression of the disease. For example, African-American female IV-drug users, once stricken with HIV, appear to have the shortest survival time of all of the major ethnic/risk groups (Rothenberg, Woelfel, Stoneburner, et al., 1987). Most AIDS patients experience a long series of increasingly debilitating infections over the course of the disease, and mortality exceeds 80 percent two years following the diagnosis of AIDS. Moreover, few patients survive more than three years after the disease has been diagnosed (Curran, Morgan, Starcher, Hardy, and Jaffe, 1985).

As HIV becomes activated in a person, the virus binds to T-4 (or "helper T") lymphocytes of the immune system, causing them to lose their normal capacity to activate other immune system cells and to die prematurely. Another type of lymphocyte, termed T-8 (or "suppressor T") cells, deactivates certain immune responses. The ratio of T-4 to T-8 cells (or helper to suppressor T cells) or the absolute number of T cells are taken as indices of immune system integrity. From this presentation it should be clear that HIV incapacitates and destroys the lymphocytes that activate the immune system, leaving intact those cells that decelerate immune system response. In spite of its lethality, HIV is surprisingly delicate and is not transmissible except in specific ways. It is present in body fluids, especially blood and semen, and transmission of the virus from an infected to a non-infected person requires that HIV-infected fluids gain direct entry into the recipient's bloodstream. In other words, HIV is transmitted by blood-to-blood contact such as would occur when drug abusers share needles, when a person is transfused with blood that is HIV-infected, when an infant is born to an HIV-infected mother, or by sexual activities in which an infected person's semen, blood, or body fluids can enter the partner's bloodstream (CDC, 1988b; 1989b).

DISEASES RELATED TO HIV INFECTION

One of the most immediate effects of HIV is to reduce the number of helper T lymphocytes. Because of this the immune system becomes less capable of resisting many infections and illnesses. In fact, many persons with immune suppression are often affected simultaneously by multiple opportunistic infections. Table 1.3 presents a description of the most common opportunistic diseases that are often associated with AIDS and HIV.

Kaposi's sarcoma (KS), first identified in the late 1800s, is a disease that primarily afflicted elderly males of Jewish or Mediterranean descent and Africans. In these populations, Kaposi's is prevalent among AIDS patients—affecting approximately 35 percent of all cases—and is also highly virulent and aggressive. Kaposi's sarcoma occurs with pneumocystic pneumonia in approximately 7 percent of AIDS patients, and Kaposi's sarcoma is more prevalent among homosexual AIDS patients than among AIDS patients from other risk groups (CDC, 1981b). Kaposi's sarcoma usually appears first as red,

Table 1.3
Diseases and Infections Commonly Associated with AIDS

	Malignancies
Kaposi's sarcoma	Lesions affecting the skin, oral mucosa, and visceral organs
Malignant lymphomas	Non-Hodgkin lymphoma most frequently affecting the central nervous system, bone marrow, and bowel
Oral, anorectal, and other malignancies	Although Kaposi's sarcoma and malignant lymphomas are the most common, increased incidence of other malignancies is also found with AIDS
	Viruses
Cytomegalovirus	Produces major organ dysfunction, often affecting gastrointestinal, adrenal, and vision systems
Herpes	Herpes simplex and zoster infections are unusually extensive and virulent in AIDS patients
Epstein-Barr virus	Produces fever, lymphadenopathy, fatigue, and other symptoms
	Protozoa
Pneumocystis carinii pneumonia	The most common opportunistic disease afflicting AIDS patients
Toxoplasma gondii	Commonly manifested clinically by encephalitis A small bowel organism producing cramps and diarrhea
	Fungi
Candida	Candida infections particularly affect mucus membranes of oral and digestive tract; respond to therapy but recur
Crytococcus neoformans	Commonly manifested clinically by meningitis
	Bacteria
Mycobacterium species	Several Mycobacterium species produce symptoms including fatigue, weight loss, and fever

purple, or blue palpable, nonpainful cutaneous tumors that occur in any body area. They often increase in number and are frequently accompanied by lymph node enlargement, fever, weight loss, and night sweats. Malignant neoplasms other than Kaposi's sarcoma also affect the central nervous system, bone marrow, and a wide range of other sites.

Pneumocystic pneumonia is the most common life-threatening opportunistic disease associated with AIDS. It is usually diagnosed in at least 60 percent of new AIDS patients (CDC, 1983) and it may be more prevalent by the ending stages of AIDS. This opportunistic disease is caused by the P carinii bacterium and is verified by laboratory tests that identify the organism in lung tissue or bronchial secretions. The mortality rate associated with this disease is about 60 percent (Kovacs and Masur, 1984). Early symptoms of this illness often include intermittent fever, chills, weight loss, cough and chest discomfort, or shortness of breath, and the acute onset of the disease in AIDS patients often follows within two to ten weeks of such symptoms (Macher and Reichert, 1984). As indicated earlier, most AIDS patients experience a long series of increasingly debilitating infections and most AIDS patients die within two years following the diagnosis.

In addition to the disease already described, a variety of other diseases are associated with AIDS and most exist concurrently with both pneumocystic pneumonia and Kaposi's sarcoma. Cytomegalovirus is a virus common in the general population, where it is usually latent. These infections spread rapidly in AIDS patients and the virus is characterized by symptoms such as fever, diarrhea, and weight loss. The virus infections produce major dysfunctions in the lungs, gastrointestinal tract, and various other organ systems. For the most part, there is no effective treatment for cytomegalovirus which results in the disease contributing to a significant number of AIDS deaths. Herpes simplex infections are common in patients with AIDS with the outbreaks being more extensive and with a higher recurrence rate among individuals with a compromised immune system than in individuals with a strong and healthy immune system. Candida infections ("thrush") are fungal in nature and primarily affect the oral cavity, esophagus, and rectum. Oral candida is evidenced by sore throat or mouth, low grade fever, pain when swallowing, or mouth ulcers. Cryptococcus infections are also a fungal disease which affects the central nervous system and often produces meningitis, encephalatis, and a variety of serious concomitant central nervous system and neurological problems. Similarly, toxoplasmosis, which is a protozoan infection can lead to similar health changes. While these infections are the most common among patients with AIDS, many more opportunistic diseases have been diagnosed in recent years. The description of these other problems goes far beyond the purpose of this book. However, it should be noted that the HIV virus is very capable of directly affecting a number of organ systems as well as the central nervous system. In fact, a large number of AIDS patients exhibit central nervous system problems which include memory loss, dementia, organic brain syndrome, and various other sensory and motor impairments (Ho, Byington, Schooley, Flynn, Rota, and Hirsh, 1985; Wolcott, 1986a, 1986b).

From the discussion above it should be obvious that there is a strong need to understand the variability of high risk sexual behaviors among African-Americans. It is my belief that this should be accomplished within the context of studies where the aims are to understand individuals within a specific race/or ethnic group rather than attempt to understand the behavior of African-Americans by comparing their behavior with information from white control groups. Unfortunately, there is a notable lack of research that specifically focuses on lifestyles and sexual behaviors that promote the transmission of HIV among young African-American adults. Similarly, very little information is available regarding factors that might be responsible for observed race/ethnic differences in AIDS knowledge or about factors that facilitate the spread of AIDS among African-Americans. One of the few studies of African-American women (Mays and Cochran, 1988) reports that 65 percent of the respondents reported no use or rare use of condoms, and that less than 25 percent used condoms during sex as a means of reducing STDs such as AIDS. Fullilove and colleagues (1990a, 1990b) note that drug use is an understudied factor which affects sexual behavior and results in poor or impaired judgement where the end result is the practice of unsafe or unprotected sexual intercourse with partners who may be at extreme risk for HIV infection. These observations are supported by studies conducted by the CDC which show interrelationships between drug use, increased sexual activity (Zabin, Hardy, Smith, and Hirsch, 1986), and STDs (Schwarcz and Rutherford, 1989).

The omission of specific information regarding the relationship between ethnicity and high risk sexual behavior related to HIV infection has made it difficult to determine the knowledge and attitudes that African-Americans, particularly individuals engaging in risky sexual behaviors, maintain about AIDS. As a consequence, much of our understanding of how to change the sexual practices, attitudes, and lifestyles of young African-Americans has been derived from a limited number of studies comparing African-Americans and whites. Even though there is a fair amount of research documenting African-American versus white differences in knowledge about AIDS and certain sexual practices, it may very well be the case that the knowledge and behavioral factors that discriminate between African-Americans and whites are different from the factors that discriminate between "high risk" and "low risk" groups within the African-American population.

It is my belief that ethnic differences may not provide much insight about the factors that predict risky sexual behaviors or those factors that are related to HIV exposure and sexually transmitted diseases within ethnic groups. It is my intention to deal further with this issue in other parts of the book (Chapter 3) because it appears that one of the major problems with our development of prevention programs is that we tend to target behaviors and attitudes that we uncover from comparing one ethnic group with another. There is basically nothing wrong with this research approach except that it may lead to a simplistic understanding of the behaviors and attitudes associated with "risky sex" within an ethnic group. Chapter 3 illustrates using data collected from African-American and white students, that the variables that should be targeted for intervention differ as a function of whether comparisons are employed between or within ethnic groups.

CHAPTER 2

Design and Methods of Inquiry

This chapter provides a description of the research design, procedures, measures of AIDS knowledge, attitudes about using condoms,
risky sexual behaviors, and statistical analyses used in this study. I
also discuss certain methodological issues that are related to this
(and other) studies. My intent in raising methodological and practical
issues is to present a context for viewing the current strengths and
reliability of the findings for this study. I hope that the problems
identified in this section will be useful for the design of future research studies among African-Americans and other groups.

The data for this book were collected as part of a larger study of
the interrelationships between drug use, attitudes and knowledge
about AIDS, and about condom usage among African-American young
adults. The participants for this inquiry were 200 African-American
males and 205 African-American females attending college in the
southern United States. Data from 74 white male and 90 white females
were also collected. For the most part, this book will focus its attention on the information obtained from the African-American subjects. The data gathered from the white students will be used at times
to facilitate the discussion of methodological issues and interpreta-
tion of findings derived from comparing ethnic groups as compared
to findings obtained from making comparisons of risk and non-risk
groups within an ethnic group. The subjects were recruited using a
number of different techniques in order to insure the participation
of African-American students in this project. The respondents recruited for this project do not represent a random sample and several
procedures were used to ascertain the sample, the most prominent
being a phone call to students from a predetermined list of all African-
American students. Approximately 85 percent of the sample was
recruited in this manner with the remaining sample being recruited

Table 2.1
Characteristics of the Sample (All Values Expressed as Percentage except Age)

	Total	Males	Females
Age (years)	21.5	22.6	20.5
Marital Status			
Single	87	87	86
Married	5	5	5
Separated/Divorced	5	4	6
Living with Significant Other	3	3	3
Education Level			
Freshman/Sophomore	65	59	70
Junior/Senior	33	38	29
Graduate School	2	2	0
Drug Usage			
Smoking			
Current	13	12	13
Ex	7	8	6
Non	80	80	81
Drinking			
Current	65	67	64
Ex	8	7	8
Non	27	26	28
Marijuana			
Current	9	13	5
Ex	11	14	8
Non	80	72	88
Crack			
Current	2	3	1
Ex	1	2	0
Non	97	95	99
Cocaine			
Current	3	3	2
Ex	1	3	1
Non	95	93	97
Sexually Transmitted Diseases			
Gonorrhea	11	18	5
Syphilis	4	7	2
Herpes	4	6	2
Genital warts	6	6	5
AIDS	4	6.5	1.5
Always used condoms during past year	28	34	21
Consider self at high risk for AIDS	13	15.5	9.5
Sexually active	85	90	80
Involved with more than 1 partner	32	47	19

by "word-of-mouth" or respondents talking to other students about the study. Several subjects were recruited through advertisements presented at social gatherings sponsored by fraternities and sororities. The subjects were administered the self-report questionnaires in small groups of five or fewer students. After the questionnaires were completed, the forms were sealed in a large envelope and a subject's number was assigned at the time the data were entered into a computer—usually within two days of data collection.

SAMPLE CHARACTERISTICS

Table 2.1 presents the characteristics of this sample of 200 African-American men and 205 African-American women. On the average, males are older than females by about two years (22.4 versus 20.5). The average age of the sample, independent of all variables, is 21.5 years. An observation of the information presented in Table 2.1 reveals that the majority of the participants were single and never married (87 percent). Most participants were within their first or second year of college (65 percent). With the exception of alcohol usage, the percentage of students who are "currently using" drugs is quite low. The data in Table 2.1 shows that 65 percent of the respondents reported that they are currently using alcohol, while 13 percent are currently smoking cigarettes. Only 9 percent of the students reported that they were currently using marijuana, while a total of 20 percent (current and ex-users) of the students have experienced marijuana. A relatively small percentage of the respondents have used crack and cocaine.

A sample of young college students have been treated previously for sexually transmitted diseases and a little more than one-quarter of the respondents (28 percent) reported that they "always" used condoms with their partner over the past 12 months. Approximately 85 percent of the respondents were sexually active at the time of the study and 32 percent were currently sexually involved with more than one partner. Nevertheless, the data shows that only 13 percent of the students consider themselves to be at high risk for HIV/AIDS.

The sample of males and females were not significantly different from each other with regards to marital status, but a slightly larger percentage of the males were juniors/seniors or enrolled in graduate studies. Rates of cigarette smoking and drinking were very similar for the sample of males and females. A significantly larger percentage of the males were currently using marijuana (13 percent versus 5 percent) or had used marijuana in the past (27 percent versus 13 percent). Whereas the percentage of males and females who were currently using crack and cocaine was exceptionally low, a significantly larger percentage of the males have used crack (5 percent versus 1 percent) and cocaine (6 percent versus 3 percent).

The data with regards to treatment for previous STDs clearly shows that a larger percentage of the males have been treated for each of the STDs. A most startling observation is that the percentage of males in this sample who have tested positive for HIV/AIDS (6.5 percent) is roughly four times higher than the percentage of females (1.5 percent). A significantly larger percentage of males than females considered themselves to be at high risk for AIDS. Similarly, a larger percentage of males were sexually active at the time of the study and more males (47 percent) than females (19 percent) were sexually involved with more than one partner. Nevertheless, condoms were always used by only 34 percent of the males and 21 percent of the females.

In summary, the demographic profile of the sample of African-American male and female college students is remarkably similar to other populations of African-American students. In general, most of the students are relatively young, single, within their freshman/sophomore years of college. However, unlike popular belief, drug use is relatively low. The information regarding the previous treatment of STDs is very similar to data gathered from several other samples of African-American adults. Finally, the information about the percentage of students who are sexually active with more than one partner is also very similar to data generated by other investigators.

MEASUREMENT INSTRUMENTS

The following self-report instruments were employed in the study, and the individual items and response formats comprising each scale can be obtained from the author.

Attitudes toward Condom Usage Questionnaire (ATCUQ)

The ATCUQ was developed by Brown (1984) to measure people's opinions about the use of condoms as contraceptive devices. The questionnaire consists of 40 questions (statements) that require the respondent to indicate whether they (1) Strongly Disagree, (2) Disagree, (3) Undecided, (4) Agree, or (5) Strongly Agree with the statements. The psychometric properties of the ATCUQ have been investigated by Brown (1984) who reported an internal consistency reliability of .93 with an average item-total correlation of .24. Item-total correlations for subjects in the present study ranged from .05 to .71 with the average being .41. The factor analysis of the ATCUQ by Brown revealed that the scale is comprised of five distinct factors. The examination of the factor structure revealed that five subscales, comprised of only 21 of the original items, could be formed. Furthermore, the items retained for the subscales had a factor loading of .35 or greater and did not load more than .25 on the other factors. Based on these criteria five subscales were formed and each measured distinctly different attitudes about the use of condoms. In addition to the five subscales, a total scale score is derived by summing responses to the 21 items. The first scale measures attitudes about condoms as a contraceptive device (Contraceptive). The scale has five items (2, 12, 34, 35, 38) and the factor loading ranged from .37 to .81 with the average being .66. Four items (14, 18, 19, 23) loaded on factor two with the average loading being .55. The items on this scale appear to be assessing whether condoms are viewed as being uncomfortable and interrupting sexual intercourse (Uncomfortable/Interrupts Sex). Factor three was comprised of five items (7, 8, 16, 24, 36) and the average factor loading was .52. The items on this factor measure attitudes about the acceptability of condoms (Acceptability). Four items (5, 11, 17, 40) loaded on factor four and the average factor loading was .61. These items tap into attitudes about how condoms add to sexual excitement (Add Excitement to Sex). Finally, factor five was comprised of three items (15, 29, 33) and the average factor loading was .60. The items on this scale appear to measure attitudes about whether condoms are inconvenient and interrupt foreplay (Inconvenient/Interrupts Foreplay).

Condoms Emotional Reactions Scale (CERS)

The CERS is a ten item self-report questionnaire that was developed by Johnson, Gant, Jackson, Gilbert, and Willis (1991a; 1991b) to measure the intensity of anger experienced in relationship to condom usage. Item total correlations for subjects in the present inquiry ranged from .43 to .71 with the average being .62. The CERS is modeled after the State Anger Scale developed by Spielberger (1988) and the State Anger Reaction Scale that was developed by Johnson (1984) (Johnson, Spielberger, Worden, and Jacobs, 1987; Johnson, Schork, and Spielberger, 1987). Both instruments measure the intensity of angry reaction experienced in stressful social situations. However, neither of the instruments included items that assessed angry reactions associated with the use (or lack of use) of condoms or other relevant behaviors during sexual intercourse.

AIDS Knowledge and Attitude Survey

This questionnaire was developed by Thomas, Gilliam, and Iwrey (1989), and consists of 101 questions regarding knowledge and attitudes about AIDS. The questions in the knowledge section addressed the following broad domains: (1) the nature of AIDS, (2) transmission of HIV, (3) risk reduction, and (4) knowledge of risk groups. The questionnaires also focused on known risk factors for HIV infection and simply asked if the respondents had ever engaged in certain risk behaviors, regardless of frequency or immediacy. Questions were presented in a forced-choice style, with response choices of "true," "false," and "do not know." A knowledge scale score was derived by summing the "correct responses" (one point each) for each of the 29 AIDS knowledge items, yielding a summary score that ranged between 0 and 29. The overall reliability of the 29 item AIDS knowledge questionnaire, using Cronbach's alpha to measure the internal consistency, was .81 for the sample of 975 African-American college students used to create the questionnaire (Thomas, Gilliam, and Iwrey, 1989). Item-total correlations for the subjects in the present inquiry ranged from .53 to .78.

Perceived Risk of Being Exposed to AIDS

This questionnaire consisted of six items which required the participants to indicate whether they were concerned about getting AIDS (i.e., I am not worried about getting AIDS; I am less likely than most people to get AIDS; I am not the kind of person who is likely to get AIDS; I consider myself to be in a high risk group for AIDS; I would rather get any other disease than AIDS; AIDS is not as big a problem as the media suggest) or considered themselves to be the kind of person to get AIDS or a member of a AIDS high risk group. Questions were presented in a forced-choice format, with response choices of "true" or "false." In addition to determining the percentage of respondents who indicated that they believed themselves to be at "increased risk," a total scale score was derived by summing the responses for each of the six questions. Higher scores are reflective of a higher "overall" perception of risk of being exposed to HIV/AIDS.

Sexually Transmitted Diseases and Sexual Behavior

The participants indicated whether they have ever been treated for sexually transmitted diseases including gonorrhea, syphilis, herpes, and genital warts. They also responded to questions which required them to indicate whether they have tested positive for HIV/AIDS. The participants also completed questions about heterosexual behaviors as well as questions about whether they have experienced anal sex, oral-genital intercourse, or whether they have experienced sexual intercourse with a prostitute. Finally, the participants completed questions about whether they "always" used condoms with their partners and other questions which addressed certain attitudes about condom usage such as whether they thought that condoms were not necessary if they loved their partner.

Drug Usage

Individual items were used to measure the frequency that several well-known drugs (i.e., alcohol, cigarettes, marijuana, crack, cocaine) are used. The questions required the respondents to indicate whether they (a) never used; (b) used, but quit; (c) use rarely; (d) use sometimes, but not daily; (e) use once a day; (f) use twice a day; (g) use five times a day; or (h) use more than five times a day. For analysis purposes, three drug use groups were created for each variable. Subjects were classified a non-user if they endorsed the (a) response, an ex-user if they endorsed the (b) response, and a current-user if they endorsed responses (c) through (h). All users were collapsed into the single groups because of the small number of subjects who reported using drugs more than once a day on a daily basis. In some analyses, the percentage of subjects in these three groups (i.e., non-users, ex-users, current-users) are compared, while other analyses treat drug use as a continuous variable. In this case, a high score is reflected of a more frequent use of the substance.

METHODOLOGICAL ISSUES AND PROBLEMS

While bisexual and homosexual contact between males and drug injection behaviors remain the most common routes of HIV transmission, the alarming rise in heterosexual transmission of HIV among African-Americans must not be ignored. Furthermore, the incredible increase in prevalence rates of sexually transmitted diseases (STDs) among African-American youth—providing yet another route of HIV transmission and infection—compounds the problem (CDC, 1988; 1988-update; CDC, 1991a; Moss and Kreiss, 1990; Moran, Aral, Jenkins, Peterman, and Alexander, 1988; Fichtner, Arao, Bount, et al., 1983; Goldsmith, 1988; Weinstein, Goodjoin, Crayton, and Lawson, 1988; Darrow, 1976). In the study described in this book we found that 13 (nine males and four females) or 4.14 percent of the 314 young adults had tested positive for AIDS, while approximately 6.25 percent of the sample have been treated for a sexually transmitted disease.

Whereas these figures appear to be a bit high, we have little cause to believe that they do not accurately reflect the extent of this problem among African-American young adults. What is most alarming about these phenomena is that STDs and AIDS remain almost entirely preventable and that the use of condoms are an effective means of preventing STDs and offer substantial protection against HIV exposure. Furthermore, as you will come to understand, the data gathered for this book suggest that African-Americans are in fact aware that these diseases are preventable with the use of condoms. Yet this study of a select population of African-American male and female college students reveals a distressing picture. In short, if college educated African-Americans (males and females) are knowledgeable about factors associated with the transmission and prevention of HIV and AIDS, why do many of them continue to engage in high risk behaviors that can lead to sterility, disfigurement, and death? It is my belief that the findings presented in this book will shed some light on this question. In this book, I have identified a relatively large group of males (47 percent) and females (19 percent) who reported that they are sexually involved with multiple partners.

As you will come to know, I discovered that African-American males differ significantly from females in their level of knowledge about AIDS, attitudes about using condoms, previous exposure to STDs, and risky sexual behaviors. A few important misperceptions that African-Americans have about the transmission of AIDS are also identified. Before I discuss these and other issues, it is important that I acknowledge several limitations of the research design and the subsequent generalizability of the findings to other groups of African-Americans.

First of all, the study that serves as the foundation for this book is correlational or cross-sectional in nature and it has many of the same difficulties as other investigations in establishing causal directions between variables (e.g., engaging in anal intercourse causes STDs). For example, I do not know if the behaviors of individuals with multiple partners (e.g., condom usage, experiencing sex with prostitutes, or having anal intercourse) occurred prior to the individuals becoming a multiple partner or after the fact. Similarly, the behavior of subjects following a positive diagnosis of HIV/AIDS is likely (I hope) to result in changes in sexual behaviors (e.g., using condoms during sexual intercourse; maintaining monogamous relationships; reductions in risky sexual behaviors such as unprotected anal intercourse) and I have no way of knowing whether the information reported for these groups was present before the diagnosis or if they reflect responses to the diagnosis of a problem.

Second, in developing the categories of multiple partners and non-multiple partners, I may have confounded monogamous relationships with serial monogamous relationships. I do not know the extent that this renders this information problematic. However, it is likely that confounding would have been demonstrated if the two groups showed fewer differences or if the pattern of differences between multiple versus non-multiple partners were not consistent for both males and females.

Third, in the present inquiry I also had some difficulties measuring certain sexual behaviors. For example, the measure of anal intercourse did not distinguish between receptive or insertive behaviors. This is important because being on the receiving end of anal intercourse carries the greatest risk for heterosexuals as well as gays. Blood vessels in tissue lining the anus and rectum are easy to rupture during anal intercourse, giving the HIV virus a direct passageway into the bloodstream. Similarly, the assessment of drug usage did not distinguish between the casual use of drugs from whether drugs were used as part of sexual foreplay or the sexual acts themselves. The measures of sexually transmitted diseases focused on previous treatment for STDs and I have no way of knowing whether the respondents currently have STDs. In general, there is also a question about the reliability of self-report data dealing with sensitive health concerns which tend to elicit socially desirable responses. Be this as it may, the pattern of the findings reported in this book are remarkably similar to observations reported in other studies where many of the above limitations were controlled. Despite changing attitudes and more permissiveness in our society, we are still faced with many situations in which it is uncomfortable to disclose information about our sexual preferences and practices.

Although several well-known researchers (Alfred Kinsey; William Masters and Virginia Johnson; Clellan Ford and Frank Beach; Paul Rozin) have been successful in collecting information about explicit sexual practices from large groups of subjects, they share a basic problem that is also relevant to the findings that make up this book. First of all, consider the nature of the subject—SEX. One's sexual behavior is usually a very private matter, and most individuals are unwilling to participate in studies of sexual attitudes and behavior. Because of this, we only know about those individuals who are willing to openly disclose this most private part of their life. In effect, therefore, none of these studies (including the present inquiry) is based on a random sample. Because of this, it is possible that the information gathered about the sexual behaviors and attitudes of people have been ascertained from groups of individuals who "might not" be representative of people in the general public.

Another problem that is common to the studies in this area is that the results are based on self-reports about topics that for most people are very private. However, for some people, the participation in a study of this type may provide an opportunity to boast about their sexual potency. In other words, some individuals may be very cordial and honest about their sexuality while others may suppress, lie, or distort the information to create a more favorable impression. However, even with these limiting factors, I have very little reason to doubt the accuracy and reliability of the data collected for this book. As indicated above, the findings may not be completely generalizable to all African-American populations and there is a serious need to conduct additional studies. One of the major strengths of this book is that it is guided by the data obtained from a sample of African-American college students. Furthermore, the discussion of the data will be guided by empirical analyses that are directed at answering specific questions about the interrelationships between risky sexual behaviors, knowledge, attitudes, drug usage, and the perception of the risk of being exposed to HIV/AIDS.

CHAPTER 3

Knowledge about AIDS among African-American Young Adults

Several studies have shown that the accuracy of knowledge about HIV and AIDS antibody status may be effective in changing risky sexual behaviors among white homosexual men (Alter and Francis, 1987; McCusker, Stoddard, Mayer, et al., 1988; Valdiserri, Lyter, Leviton, et al., 1988). However, it has been indicated that the findings derived from these studies may be, at best, marginally applicable to African-American populations. There is no doubt that it is important to determine the extent of knowledge and misinformation about HIV and AIDS that is present in specific populations, particularly African-Americans and Hispanics. The determination of changes in knowledge and attitudes over time will enable researchers to develop educational interventions that focus both on the specific information deficits and the unique attitudinal barriers that are unique to the specific population group. Without a strategy of this nature we will not have a sound foundation for the development, modification, or implementation of AIDS prevention programs that are appropriate and sensitive to the behaviors and attitudes of specific ethnic groups.

As of 1991, there was a notably small number of research projects concerning interrelationships between AIDS knowledge, attitudes, and behavior that focused on African-American populations. In the mid to late 1980s, several studies were conducted to compare knowledge, attitudes, and sexual behaviors of African-Americans, whites, and other ethnic groups. DiClemente, Boyer, and Morales (1988) reported on knowledge about the cause of AIDS transmission, attitudes, and misperceptions among African-American and Latino adolescents.

Included in this sample were 261 (42 percent) white, 226 (36 percent) African-American, and 141 (22 percent) Latino adolescents who were residents of the San Francisco Unified School District. The average age of the students was 16 years and 51.8 percent of the sample were male. The results of this study revealed that African-American and Latino adolescents were approximately twice as likely as white adolescents to have misperceptions about the causal transmission of AIDS.

Adolescents with lower levels of knowledge about AIDS, irrespective of ethnic group membership, were more likely to perceive themselves at high risk for contracting AIDS. Substantial ethnic differences were also found in the knowledge of AIDS. Whereas all ethnic groups correctly reported that "having sex with someone who has AIDS is one way of getting the disease" and were aware that sharing intravenous needles with drug users was also a major mode of disease transmission, a greater proportion of white adolescents (72 percent) were aware that using condoms during sexual intercourse would lower the risk of disease transmission compared with 60 percent of the African-American and 58 percent of the Latino adolescents. Both African-Americans and Latino adolescents were less likely than whites to respond correctly to the statement that "all gay men have AIDS." Although African-Americans were more knowledgeable than their Latino peers, these investigators feel that both groups may be at increased risk for AIDS transmission as a consequence of risky sexual practices due to insufficient information. It is interesting that this conclusion was derived from the fact that African-Americans and Latinos exhibited greater knowledge deficits than whites rather than from determining the relationship between knowledge about AIDS and risky sexual behaviors and practices for each of the specific ethnic groups.

In another study by DiClemente, Zorn, and Temoshook (1986) a total of 1,326 adolescents were examined to determine whether there were ethnic differences in knowledge and attitudes. The adolescent sample was comprised of 19 percent white, 17 percent African-American, 49 percent Asian, and 11 percent Hispanic students enrolled in Family Life Education classes at ten high schools in the San Francisco Unified School District. Basically, the results of this investigation revealed that AIDS-related knowledge was typically quite good. For example, with respect to disease transmission, 92 percent of the students correctly indicated that "sexual intercourse was one mode of contracting AIDS." On the other hand, only 60 percent were aware that "use of condoms during sexual intercourse may lower the risk of getting the disease." This large discrepancy suggests that a large segment of the adolescent sample, while knowing a major route of disease transmission, will nonetheless engage in unprotected sexual intercourse.

The majority of adolescents in this study were aware that receiving blood from a transfusion (84 percent) or sharing intravenous needles (81 percent) were also major routes of disease transmission. There were a number of important areas where the students were quite uninformed. For example, only 66 percent were aware that AIDS could not be spread by using someone's personal belongings and only 68 percent knew that engaging in casual contact (i.e., shaking hands) would not lead to contracting the disease. Less than half of the students (41 percent) correctly reported that kissing was not a route of AIDS transmission. Interestingly enough, a large percent of the adolescents (74 percent) were worried about contracting the disease and 79 percent were afraid of getting AIDS. Overall, AIDS-related knowledge was lower among African-Americans and the other ethnic groups compared to whites. Moreover, a lower level of knowledge was significantly correlated with an increased perception of personal susceptibility. Similar findings were reported by Seltzer, Gilliam, and Stroman (1988) for a sample of 489 residents of the District of Columbia. In other words, individuals who had the lowest AIDS-related knowledge were more likely to be less educated, African-American, and to have a greater personal concern for contracting AIDS.

A rather interesting and important study was reported by Thomas, Gilliam, and Iwrey (1989). The subjects for this investigation were 975 undergraduates attending a large East Coast university during the 1987/88 academic school year. Of the participants, 94 percent were African-American, while 61 percent were women and 39 percent were men. The average age was 21 years and most students were single (95 percent). In general, the knowledge regarding basic facts about AIDS was very satisfactory with the students correctly responding on average to 82 percent of the questions (20.5 out of 25 questions) concerning knowledge about the nature of AIDS. On the other hand, the examination of the knowledge scores for students who reported that they engage in high-risk behaviors (anal intercourse, previous treatment for STD, multiple sex partners, heroine use) provided great cause for concern.

Individuals who participated in these high-risk behaviors knew significantly less about AIDS than students who did not participate in high-risk behaviors. In other words, the results of this study show that low knowledge scores among the group of African-American college students were statistically different for the high-risk versus low-risk groups. However, it is uncertain whether knowledge about AIDS was statistically correlated with high-risk sexual behaviors or simply different for the high-risk versus low-risk group. Be this as it may, the study by Thomas and his associates is extremely important because it suggests that lack of knowledge is associated with risky sexual behaviors among African-Americans.

Overall, the results of this study support the need to increase efforts to deliver effective AIDS prevention and HIV risk-reduction information to African-American college students. The findings also suggest that the delivery of AIDS information needs to specifically target individuals who may be engaged in behaviors that place them at increased risk for HIV infection and AIDS. It is also important to note that although men represented only 39 percent of the sample, they were overrepresented among students who had used heroin (45 percent), had multiple sex partners (55 percent), and had been treated for an STD (45 percent). Furthermore, it should be recalled that AIDS knowledge was significantly lower for African-American students who used heroin, had multiple sex partners, and had been treated for an STD. As a consequence, African-American males in this study were less knowledgeable about AIDS than African-American females. This observation is consistent with most findings which show that African-American males represent one of the most difficult groups to reach with effective AIDS education. It is also possible that this situation will continue as long as AIDS is perceived as a "gay" disease.

An earlier study by Seltzer and Smith (1988) supports the need for more detailed investigations of attitudes/knowledge about AIDS and condom usage among African-American groups at high risk for HIV infection. Data obtained from their large national survey of 1,095 residents (214 were African-American, 770 were white, and 111 belonged to other racial groups) were derived from a survey conducted by the Times-Mirror Company in 1987 and the sampling frame included all telephone residents in the nation. To make reasonable estimates about areas where the risk of AIDS is elevated, five metropolitan areas—Los Angeles, San Francisco, New York City, Miami, and New Jersey—were included as individual strata. Taken together, these cities account for three-fifths of all AIDS cases. Included in the survey were questions about AIDS knowledge and sexual behaviors. The first question about AIDS knowledge asked respondents to assess their own level of knowledge.

The results of this investigation indicated that while whites had greater knowledge and held less misconceptions about AIDS, significant differences between African-American and white respondents disappeared once the education level of the respondents were considered. Moreover, respondents with higher education (regardless of ethnicity) reported the most accurate knowledge about AIDS and were less likely to believe that AIDS could be transmitted from food or toilet seats. Among African-American respondents, there was no significant relationship between gender and AIDS knowledge. There were no significant differences between African-Americans and whites regarding whether or not they believed that HIV could be transmitted via food. However, African-American respondents were more likely than whites to believe that HIV could be transmitted via toilet seats (25 percent versus 19 percent). African-Americans were more likely than whites to say that they were more afraid of getting AIDS compared to numerous other diseases (59 percent versus 28 percent).

African-Americans were also more likely than whites to say they were at low risk for being exposed to HIV/AIDS (81 percent versus 91 percent), while white respondents were more likely than African-Americans to report that AIDS had no impact on their lifestyles (66 percent versus 50 percent). Finally, African-Americans were more likely than whites to report two or more sex partners in the past year (22 percent versus 11 percent). Among white respondents, those with multiple sex partners were better able to assess their own risk compared to respondents without multiple sex partners (24 percent versus 7 percent). However, among African-Americans there was no corresponding relationship between multiple sex partnership and perceived risk for AIDS. Interestingly enough, only 24 percent of the total sample who had not bought condoms during the past year said their risk was high. Among respondents with multiple sex partners, 53 percent of the whites and 45 percent of the African-Americans reported buying condoms within the past year. Although there were ethnic differences in attitudes about the use of condoms and sex within or outside monogamous relationships, a more thorough investigation of these factors among African-Americans may provide information that is necessary for the development of effective AIDS prevention programs for African-American adults.

In the last two to four years a number of other studies have examined the relationships between AIDS-related knowledge and risky sexual behavior among young adults. While the majority of these studies have included African-Americans and other ethnic minority groups, few of the studies have determined whether relationships between knowledge and risky sexual behavior vary as a function of ethnicity. For example, Roscoe and Kruger (1990) determined whether knowledge about AIDS was related to sexual behavior among a sample of 166 females and 89 male university students. The results of this study indicated that 33 percent of the females and 37 percent of the males had made significant changes in their sexual behavior because of the threat of AIDS. In another study (Baldwin and Baldwin, 1988), the aim was to determine whether 171 students who were "virgin" differed from 627 "nonvirgins" in their knowledge about AIDS and fears about contracting AIDS. The sample included 84 percent white, 2.2 percent African-American, 5.6 percent Hispanic, and 7.9 percent Asian students. In general, there was no significant difference between virgins and nonvirgins in their knowledge about AIDS. However, students with the greatest knowledge about AIDS use less caution about engaging in sexual relationships, and less than 20 percent of the sexually active students reported using condoms 75 percent of the time or more in the last three months. Interestingly enough, females were significantly more likely than males to be cautious about sexual encounters and to ask their sexual partners about their past AIDS-related activities. While there was no significant relationship between the number of current sexual partners and AIDS-related knowledge, subjects with multiple sex partners were more worried about contracting AIDS. Nevertheless, only 2.5 percent of the subjects with three or more partners in the last three months used condoms 75 percent of the time or more. The findings in this study also revealed that the more religious students had significantly less accurate knowledge about AIDS, but the religious students were not significantly different from the less religious students when it came to sexual behaviors. In neither of these studies did the investigators determine whether the findings differ as a function of ethnicity.

Although a number of professionals have targeted health education as a method of reducing the risk of HIV transmission among adolescents/young adults (e.g., DiClemente, 1989; Brown and Fritz, 1988), it is not clear whether intervention procedures to increase knowledge about AIDS is sufficient to effect changes in risky sexual behavior. Some researchers (Rickert, Gottlieb, and Jay, 1990; Kegeles, Adler, and Irwin, 1988; Roscoe and Kruger, 1990; Baldwin and Baldwin, 1988a; Strunin and Hingson, 1987; Thurman and Franklin, 1990) have found that a high degree of knowledge about the cause of AIDS and transmission modes does not correlate with changes in sexual practices. However, the research of other investigators (Turner et al., 1988; Manning, Barenberg, Gallese, and Rice, 1989; Ishii-Kuntz, 1988) supports the notion that increasing AIDS knowledge has a direct effect upon risk-reduction activities in adolescents and young adults.

Roscoe and Krueger's (1990) random mail survey of AIDS knowledge and behavior change among 166 females and 89 males yielded results consistent with other literature which documents the high degree of knowledge about AIDS in young adults. They found that over 90 percent of their sample of junior and senior level college students answered two-thirds of questions assessing knowledge about AIDS correctly. Sex differences were found in that significantly more females knew that women were not more likely to get AIDS during their period, whereas more males knew that the cause of AIDS had been found. Also consistent with prior research, these investigators found that on average only 34 percent of their participants (37 percent of males and 33 percent of females) changed their sexual behavior in response to the AIDS threat. However, these researchers noted that they did not assess the sexual practices of these students before the AIDS scare. Therefore, it is possible that the 66 percent who did not report behavior change had already made changes in their sexual behaviors.

Another likely alternative is that these individuals, like those in other research studies, do not view AIDS as a personal problem. Whereas the large majority of those who reported changing behavior stated that they were more selective in their choice of a partner, the process of "being more selective" about the choice of the partners appears to have a few problems. For example, a large number of these students reported that they look for signs of physical manifestations of the disease in others and believe that if the person they are with is nice he/she will not have AIDS. These are obvious misconceptions and myths that could put individuals at risk despite how selective they believe themselves to be. In general, these observations suggests that to a certain extent public-health information is reaching young adults, but we are not doing a great job impacting young adults to question the accuracy of their knowledge about factors related to the transmission of HIV/AIDS. Moreover, these data also suggest that there is a need to educate and inform young adults about particular myths (e.g., if he/she looks healthy the chances are low that they have HIV/AIDS; if he/she is well-educated the chances are low that they have HIV/AIDS) associated with making choices about sexual partners.

Additional research demonstrating the incongruency between AIDS knowledge and safe sexual practices was conducted using a sample of 851 undergraduates at a university in southern California. Knowledge of AIDS was assessed by 19 questions which focused on the modes of transmission while sexual practices were assessed through questions asking if subjects were limiting their number of sexual partners, using caution about the people they had sex with, getting to know a partner longer before sex, and avoiding or decreasing vaginal sex due to concern about AIDS. Other questions regarding safer sexual practices focused on the extent that potential partners were questioned about their drug use, history of STDs, and past sexual behavior. Those who engaged in sex within the last three months were also questioned about frequency of condom use.

The results of this study indicated that those subjects who reported having a new partner within the last three months were no less knowledgeable about AIDS, but worried more about contracting it, asked their partners less questions regarding past sexual history and health practices, and used condoms less frequently than students who were not involved in new relationships. Furthermore, there was no significant relationship between multiple partnerships and knowledge about AIDS. Again, as with the students engaged in new sexual relationships, those with multiple partners were not cautious about their sexual encounters nor did they ask their partners about their past sexual history despite being more worried about contracting AIDS than their less active peers. In addition, condom usage was quite low among those individuals who were engaging in sex with numerous partners. Only 2.5 percent of those with three or more partners used condoms 75 percent of the time or more. Due to the small number of African-Americans in the study, analyses of ethnicity were inappropriate (Baldwin and Baldwin, 1988a). However, additional research conducted by Baldwin and Baldwin (1988b) revealed that 66 percent of students engaging in vaginal intercourse within the last three months did not use condoms and that Hispanics were more likely than any other ethnic group to use condoms. Another frightening finding was that 19 percent of students who had intercourse within the last three months did so with a stranger or casual acquaintance. Not surprisingly, females were significantly more cautious about their sexual behaviors than males.

A random sample of 829 adolescents, age 16 to 19, was used to collect data about AIDS knowledge, beliefs, and sexual behaviors related to AIDS (Strunin and Hingson, 1987). The data was collected using a telephone survey and 86 percent of the adolescents were sexually active. Strunin and Hingson (1987) found that only 20 percent of these sexually active teenagers changed their behavior in ways that are effective to reduce the risk of exposure to HIV/AIDS. Ten percent reported using condoms while an additional 10 percent stated they now abstained from sex. Approximately 60 percent of the remaining students stated they were more careful or more selective of their sexual partners. Interestingly enough, 54 percent of the students were not worried about contracting AIDS while 22 percent of the students were either somewhat concerned or worried a great deal about being exposed to HIV/AIDS. Depending upon the criteria these subjects use for selectivity (e.g., if he/she looks healthy they don't have HIV/AIDS), they may still be at increased risk for being exposed to HIV and AIDS.

Although knowledge about HIV/AIDS was relatively high in this sample, 8 percent of subjects did not know AIDS could be contracted through heterosexual contact. Another 15 percent did not know that it could be transmitted through vaginal fluids where 14 percent believed that it simply could not. Over half (60 percent) thought giving blood was a mode of transmission while 22 percent were unaware that AIDS could be transmitted through semen. Even though these deficiencies in knowledge suggest that education may heighten these adolescents' awareness of the necessary precautions needed to be taken for protection against HIV infection, the high degree of knowledge and lack of behavior change again suggests that educational efforts are not too effective in causing young adults to change risky sex behaviors. Perhaps a more effective educational campaign should be multimodal, focusing on more than providing information about the disease. As indicated earlier, our primary prevention messages need to effectively transmit accurate information as well as elicit an optimal level of anxiety and worry to motivate individuals to assess and evaluate their own behavior. Ideally these sources of information should cause individuals to, upon questioning their own risk, alter their sexual behaviors to lower their own risk of being exposed to HIV/AIDS.

Consistent with the aforementioned point, telephone interviews of undergraduates attending the University of Massachusetts (Thurman and Franklin, 1990) revealed that more than 80 percent of respondents were highly knowledgeable about the factors associated with the transmission and prevention of AIDS. In general, relatively few people in this sample were misinformed about AIDS. Although 96 percent viewed condoms as an effective means for risk reduction and 87 percent believed limiting the number of sexual partners could reduce risk, 57 percent of students reported they had not changed their behavior in response to the AIDS epidemic. This may be attributable to the fact that although 61 percent of students feared a campus-wide spread of the AIDS virus, only 18 percent felt personally susceptible to infection.

Taking a different approach, Manning, Barenberg, Gallese, and Rice (1989) developed a questionnaire for college students about AIDS and safer sex based upon the Health Belief Model (HBM). This model has five major dimensions which include (1) perceived susceptibility to AIDS, (2) perceived seriousness of contracting AIDS, (3) perceived benefit of a particular health action, (4) perceived barriers to practicing safe sex, and (5) perceived likelihood of adhering to a recommended health action. The HBM requires that all components are present if behavior is to change. The perceived barrier component which is the individuals' assessment of the costs and benefits of a health action played a major role in this study. The subjects in this study were 106 female and 43 male undergraduates who were seeking medical attention at the student health center while attending summer school. The majority of students were white (83 percent), with African-Americans comprising 9 percent and Hispanics and

Asians making up the other 8 percent of the students. The results of this investigation revealed that although overall knowledge about AIDS was high, there were some individuals who were deficient in AIDS knowledge. Furthermore, by classifying these individuals into groups based upon whether they were high in knowledge (correctly answering 92 percent of knowledge questions or better) or low in knowledge (correctly answering 83 percent and below), researchers were able to discriminate between those who felt the barriers to safer sex were high from those who did not. Specifically, they found that low scorers on knowledge perceived the costs of practicing safe sex to outweigh the benefits significantly more than the high scorers. It appears that low scorers would rather deal with present problems than spend time in retrospection or projecting into the future. These researchers feel that targeting these aspects of the HBM will lead to safer sexual practices, emphasizing that high scores on other components in isolation is not sufficient for behavior change. The investigators concluded that the failure to practice safe sex despite having accurate knowledge about the transmission of AIDS may be due to egocentricity.

DOES INCREASING AIDS KNOWLEDGE DECREASE RISKY SEXUAL BEHAVIORS?

Although the literature reviewed thus far suggests that AIDS knowledge is not correlated with changes in sexual behaviors, some research suggests that in various cases it is effective in motivating some individuals to engage in safer sexual practices. In one survey of both 288 undergraduates and 86 post-graduates attending Oxford University, researchers found overall knowledge about AIDS to be high (Turner et al., 1988). Of the 374 students who participated in this investigation, 127 were female while 247 were male, and the majority of students were single (365 out of 374). Furthermore, of those who experienced intercourse, 35 percent of the women and 44 percent of the men stated they had been more likely to use a condom due to fear of AIDS and 31 percent of this group were using condoms as their most frequent form of contraception. Of those who had not changed their use of condoms, only 2 percent were using it as a primary method of contraception.

Although there was no correlation between increased condom use and multiple partnerships in this sample, 49 percent of the women and 30 percent of the men stated they had or would have fewer sexual partners because of AIDS risk (Turner et al., 1988). Of the 20 percent who described themselves at "average risk" of being exposed to HIV/

AIDS, 50 percent had experienced sexual intercourse with more than three partners. Of the 78 percent who described themselves as being at "lower than average risk," 14 percent had experienced sexual intercourse with more than three partners. In contrast, 7 out of the 11 students who described themselves as being at "higher than average risk" had experienced sexual intercourse with more than three partners. Although these researchers feel that this study provides support that AIDS knowledge may lead to changes in sexual behavior, approximately two-thirds of the subjects did not report changes in contraceptive methods or intent to change with regard to sexual practices. This observation is consistent with research documenting the poor association between risky sexual behaviors and AIDS knowledge. In summary, this research suggests that the perception of vulnerability may have a mediating role wherein those individuals who have accurate knowledge of AIDS and feel vulnerable to the illness appear to be more likely to change risky sexual behavior patterns than those who are either deficient in knowledge or feel invulnerable to AIDS.

In a study examining the effects of increasing knowledge and concern about AIDS on perceived changes in sexual practices, Ishii-Kuntz (1988) found that with the exception of condom use, college females were more likely to report changes in their sexual behavior than college males. The sample consisted of 135 males and 167 females, all of whom were sexually active and the majority (93 percent) were under age 24. Approximately half (52 percent) of the females were more likely to date longer before engaging in sexual intercourse, and 55 percent were more likely to ask potential sex partners about their past sexual history compared to 24.6 percent and 33.1 percent of males.

The results of this study also revealed that 79 percent of these subjects with a history of homosexual experiences reported that they were more likely to increase the length of time between meeting a possible sexual partner and having intercourse with this partner. Among those very concerned about AIDS, 83 percent reported that they ask potential partners about their sex history compared to 61 percent of those individuals not concerned about contracting AIDS. Although the overall pattern of these data suggests that knowledge impacts behavior, this study also revealed that knowledge about AIDS neither increased condom usage or decreased high-risk sexual behavior such as oral and anal sex. Basically, individuals who are more concerned about contracting HIV/AIDS were more likely to use a condom and less likely to engage in unprotected oral or anal sex.

In a comparison of two educational programs about AIDS in African-American and white female adolescents (Rickert, Gottlieb, and Jay,

1990), it was found that knowledge about AIDS was higher in the groups who received education either through a lecture about AIDS, or a combined lecture and videotape demonstrating the purpose and use of condoms, than in a control group which did not receive any educational information. However, the two groups that received education did not differ from one another with regard to knowledge, and did not significantly differ from one another or the control group with regard to attitudes toward practicing preventative behaviors or willingness to acquire free condoms. Secondary analyses did show, however, that the educational program using both a lecture and videotape had a significant impact on those students who had a prior history of purchasing condoms. These individuals were more likely to utilize the free condoms than other students who only received the lecture. These data suggest that AIDS prevention efforts may be more effective if the format for educating individuals takes into consideration information about previous sexual behaviors and attitudes about preventative sexual practices that may already be in place such as as a prior history of using condoms.

Using a different research methodology, other investigators (Kegeles, Adler, and Irwin, 1988) have assessed whether knowledge and attitude regarding condoms as a means of prevention against STDs in adolescents (age 14–19 years) change over a year. In this research, the specific areas examined were knowledge that condoms prevent STDs, the value placed on contraceptives which prevent STDs, the importance of using contraceptives which prevent STDs, intentions to use condoms, and finally intentions to use condoms most of the time. Results of this study showed that the majority of adolescents had previously been involved with multiple sexual partners. Approximately 40 percent of the women and 69 percent of the men had more than one sexual partner during the year following the initial assessment. Furthermore, of those who reported being sexually active a month prior to both the first and second survey, only 27 percent of the women and 41 percent of the men reported using condoms at the time of the first survey and 23 percent of the women and 49 percent of the men reported using them a month prior to the second survey.

What is most startling is that less than 2.5 percent of the women and a little over 8 percent of the men reported "always" using condoms during the study year. Overall, the importance placed upon condoms for preventing STD transmission was high. However, condom importance decreased in women over the year and in both surveys women showed little intention to have their partners use condoms. The intention to use condoms decreased in men over the survey year. Although all ethnic groups were represented in this study, analyses were not conducted by race. The researchers note that these findings are alarming given that the survey was conducted in an area where school and media coverage of AIDS increased over time. Therefore, they concluded that information dissemination may not reduce risk in adolescents, but perhaps efforts should be targeted towards perceptions of personal vulnerability to acquiring AIDS/HIV infections (Kegeles, Adler, and Irwin, 1988). The idea behind this approach is that the acquisition and performance of many behaviors is motivated by the presence of an optimal level of anxiety, fear, and worry. For example, in the case of a student studying for an examination, an excessively high level of anxiety, fear, and worry will most likely be associated with procrastination and ultimately poor test performance regardless of the amount of time put into studying for the exam. On the other hand, the student who does not experience anxiety is likely to not even prepare for the exam because of a number of different reasons (e.g., a belief that the exam will be easy) and consequently perform poorly on the exam. In contrast to both of these styles are individuals with a moderate and optimal level of anxiety which is almost used as fuel to motivate the individual to study and prepare for the examination as if they were preparing for a battle. One of the consequences of studying for the examination will be a reduction in anxiety, enhanced comfort, and confidence that the examination can be successfully completed.

Unfortunately, the level of motivational anxiety and fear within our public health messages concerning HIV/AIDS has been unsteady and it is difficult to judge whether the reasons for their ineffectiveness among African-Americans is a consequence of too much or too little anxiety and fear about one's own personal vulnerability.

As indicated earlier, only a few documented studies have investigated AIDS knowledge among African-American groups (Jaffe, Seehaus, Wagner, and Leadbeater, 1988; DiClemente, Zorn, and Temoshok, 1987; DiClemente, Boyer, and Morales, 1988; Bell, Feraios, and Bryan, 1990; Johnson et al., 1992; Thomas, Gilliam, and Iwrey, 1989). A study (Bell, Feraios, and Bryan, 1990) of the interrelationships among overall knowledge about AIDS, attitudes about sexuality, drugs, AIDS, and related aspects of one's social world was investigated among four groups of adolescent males: African-Americans ($n = 26$), whites ($n = 19$), Puerto Ricans ($n = 15$), and Mexicans ($n = 18$). All subjects were between 15 and 19 years old and enrolled in high schools in high stress environments (e.g., low socioeconomic and high crime areas) where the dropout rate from school was higher than 60 percent.

Results of this investigation revealed that whites were most knowledgeable, followed by Puerto Ricans, African-Americans, and Mexicans. The exceptions to this were in the cases where Puerto Ricans were deficient in knowledge of casual contact and where both Puerto Ricans and whites knew more miscellaneous facts about AIDS than Mexicans. Knowledge about AIDS appeared to be enhanced by the number of sources these adolescents used to get their information about AIDS. The number of sources did not vary by race, but on an individual level evidence suggests that those who supplemented their information about AIDS by having a larger number of sources had a better knowledge of how AIDS was transmitted intravenously. Talking about AIDS with others and knowing more gay people were both associated with greater knowledge of AIDS. Finally, subjects who reported a greater degree of "hearing about AIDS" in the newspaper, magazines, television, or from friends reported a greater amount of anger and fear of homosexuals and IV-drug users. Moreover, these individuals also perceived AIDS to be a problem involving other people and not themselves.

In a research study of predominantly African-American (47 percent) and Hispanic (44 percent) adolescent females (ages 13 to 21), researchers found that although knowledge of AIDS was accurate, most respondents did not report changes in their sexual practices to avoid getting AIDS. Over 25 percent of the sample acknowledged having anal intercourse, with 68 percent of these individuals having engaged in anal intercourse within the preceding three months. There was no significant difference between African-Americans and Hispanics in the incidence of anal sex. Oral sex was practiced by 48 percent of the sexually active girls, and there was a trend for this behavior as well as knowledge about AIDS to increase with age.

As far as condom use is concerned, condoms were less likely to be used during anal intercourse than vaginal intercourse and attitudes about them were mixed. Of the 111 sexually active females, 45 percent of the sample agreed that condoms reduce sexual pleasure too much while 56 percent disagreed with this statement (Jaffe, Seehaus, Wagner, and Leadbeater, 1988). Although age was related to having experiences with oral and anal intercourse, no significant relationships were found between age and worry about contracting HIV/AIDS. Be this as it may, 10 percent of this sample of females "worried all the time," and 7.2 percent "worried often" about being exposed to HIV/AIDS.

In a self-report questionnaire study of students representing white, African-American, Asian, and Hispanic ethnic groups, DiClemente, Zorn, and Temoshok (1987) found deficits in knowledge with regard to casual contact with AIDS victims. Although 92 percent were aware that sexual intercourse with an infected person was one means of transmitting the disease, only 74 percent correctly knew that AIDS was an immune-deficiency disease, and 60 percent were unsure that it is caused by a virus. Many respondents were not aware that AIDS could not be transmitted through kissing or touching, and 40 percent did not know or were unsure that condoms would reduce the risk of contracting the disease. Ethnic differences in knowledge were found with whites being more knowledgeable than African-Americans, Asians, and Hispanics. In addition, African-Americans were more knowledgeable than Asians, but no differences were found between African-Americans and Hispanics.

Further validating the misconceptions that minorities may have regarding AIDS, Thomas, Gilliam, and Iwrey (1989) found that out of 975 predominantly African-American students, over 90 percent had accurate knowledge regarding the basic facts about AIDS that had received media attention, and knew about the different modes of AIDS transmission. However, less than 80 percent knew that HIV is not the same virus as the herpes virus and that symptoms of AIDS require more than 12 to 24 hours to appear. Less than 30 percent knew that the AIDS virus is not transmitted by insects and less than 80 percent knew that AIDS is not transmitted on toilet seats, by kissing, or by coughing. These misconceptions about AIDS are consistent with research conducted by other investigators using white populations. For example, a study by Winslow (1988) of undergraduate students attending San Diego State University found that students feared that AIDS could be transmitted through heterosexual intercourse, kissing, drinking from the same glass, and eating food that had been prepared by a person with HIV/AIDS. In addition, another study confirmed that although some students possess a moderate degree of knowledge about AIDS, they are least knowledgeable about the prevalence of AIDS in the United States and the low degree of risk for acquiring AIDS associated with in-hospital blood transfusions.

In summary, the findings in this section indicate that there is tremendous variability in the level of knowledge that African-Americans have about AIDS. The level of knowledge does not appear to be uniformly lower among African-Americans compared to other ethnic groups. However, regardless of ethnicity, having a good knowledge about AIDS does not appear to be significantly related to lower levels of risky sexual behavior. In other words, knowledge about AIDS does not appear to be a significant predictor of risky sexual behavior among African-American young adults or other ethnic groups.

HOW WELL DOES KNOWLEDGE PREDICT RISKY SEXUAL BEHAVIORS AMONG AFRICAN-AMERICANS?

The findings derived from the data collected for this book revealed that knowledge about AIDS was exceptionally high among both the male and female students. In general, knowledge about AIDS was not significantly related to years in college, age, or marital status.

Table 3.1
Correlations between AIDS Knowledge and Sexual Behaviors/Attitudes

Variables	Total Sample	Males	Females
Sex with male	-.12*	.15*	-.11
Sex with female	.06	-.18**	.03
Sexually active	.14**	.20**	.11
Anal sex	.06	.06	.01
Oral sex	-.04	-.08	-.02
Sex with prostitute	-.16**	.13#	.01
Four or more partners in past year	.05	-.06	.08
Perceived risk	-.02	-.00	-.03
Member of AIDS risk group	.09#	.11	.03
Condoms should be used during sex	.18***	.22**	-.02
Always used condoms	.01	.01	-.07
Gonorrhea	.06	-.01	.04
Syphilis	-.21***	-.22***	.11#
Herpes	-.13**	-.18**	.01
Genital warts	-.12*	-.11	.12#
HIV/AIDS	-.33***	-.42***	.07

$\#p < .10; *p < .05; **p < .01; ***p < 001.$

On average, the sample of students correctly answered 24 out of the 29 AIDS knowledge questions. The only demographic factor that was significantly related to AIDS knowledge was gender. Males scored significantly lower (average score = 23.35 + 5.95) on the AIDS knowledge questionnaire than females (average score = 24.15 + 2.85). For males, the major AIDS knowledge deficits consisted of very basic information about the transmission of AIDS (e.g., you can get AIDS from having sex with someone who has AIDS: 90 percent correct for males and 99 percent correct for females; receiving a blood transfusion with infected blood can give you AIDS: 89 percent correct for males and 99 percent correct for females; you can get AIDS by sharing a needle with a drug user who has the disease: 96 percent correct for males and 100 percent correct for females). The data presented in Table 3.1 show the correlations between knowledge scores, various measures of sexual behavior, and attitudes for the total sample as well as for males and females. As can be observed, knowledge about AIDS for the total sample was significantly correlated with being sexually active, experiencing sex with a prostitute, and the belief that condoms should be used during sexual intercourse. Having a low level of AIDS knowledge was also significantly related to having a history of syphilis, herpes, genital warts, and testing positive for HIV/AIDS. Interestingly enough, the data in Table 3.1 shows that the percentage of African-American males with a history of these STDs was not significantly higher than the African-American females. It should be noted, however, that low AIDS knowledge is significantly related to having a history of sexually transmitted diseases and testing positive for HIV/AIDS only among African-American males. Therefore, the overall pattern of the data collected from my sample of African-American college students indicate that knowledge about AIDS is significantly related to certain risky sexual behaviors, but only among African-American males. Interestingly enough, African-American males, on average, know significantly less about factors related to AIDS transmission than African-American females.

CHAPTER 4

Multiple Sex Partners and Risky Sexual Behavior

Early in the 1970s, Robert Staples published two articles in a journal called the *Black Scholar* ("The myth of Black sexual superiority: A reexamination" and "The Black-American Family in Evolutionary Perspective") in which he concluded that because of the absence of available men, it is impossible for every African-American woman to be in a monogamous relationship. This fact alone, he believed, would force African-American people to adopt alternative family lifestyles. The data available at the time showed that as of 1976, the majority of African-American women between the ages of 20 and 45 were not married and living with a spouse. In 1975, 27 percent of the African-American population between the ages of 25 and 54 were divorced, compared with only 8 percent of whites in the same age group. The problem of low sex ratio (proportion of males to females) has been ignored by most social scientists. However, it appears that the marriage rates are directly related to sex ratio. Even though the sex ratio is relatively even at ages 14 to 17, by the ages of 30 to 34 there are only 77 African-American men for every 100 African-American women. Also, after age 24, at every age period among African-Americans there is a higher percentage of men than women who are married with a spouse present.

For the African-American community, it is very apparent that the "family" is very fragile and under siege. Female-headed households are nearing the 50 percent mark, and significantly more African-American children are born into poverty than any other group of children. African-American men are unemployed, imprisoned, murdered (i.e., black-on-black crime), addicted to drugs, or eliminated through various wars with other nations as well as gang wars, or through poor medical care at rates that are staggering given their proportion in the total population. In the words of Chicago writer, publisher, and activist Haki Madhubuti, Black-America is "basically at war," and the major casualties have been our relationships and our families. The shortages of men that we have today may be accidental or a direct relationship to institutional racism. Nevertheless, when women and children exist in a world ruled by men and they don't have men to look up to as role models, we have the right atmosphere for a high level of anxiety, irritability, depression, suicide, and confusion about sex role identities. It is within this confused atmosphere that the idea of sharing men or engaging in multiple sexual relationships has surfaced as an alternative to how African-American men and women can mingle. In fact, there are new arguments being put forth these days to support the idea that African-American women have no alternative other than sharing a man. While many of these arguments have become myths, some of them are very important and very real. For example, it has been argued that the reason for the sharing of men is that there is a shortage of African-American men.

According to the 1989 U.S. Census Bureau figures, among non-married African-Americans ages 18 to 39 there were 3,654,000 women compared to 3,352,000 men. This computes to 92 available African-American men for every 100 women—eight fewer men. As you can tell, this ratio does not indicate that there is a huge shortage of African-American men. However, when we consider whether the African-American men are desirable and functioning the distributions becomes very skewed. In other words, when we consider the proportion of African-American men who are incarcerated, addicted to drugs, homosexual, select white women as partners, or who are uneducated and unemployable, it becomes very clear that there is a very real shortage of African-American men. Given the numbers, it is very possible that some African-American women will never marry and conceive children with an African-American male who is part of a monogamous relationship. It is apparent that African-American women may not have much of an option to pick and choose a partner like the male does. The most current data on this topic indicates that approximately 55 percent of all African-American births annually are out-of-wedlock. Given the shortage of "good" African-American men, and the strong possibility that out-of-wedlock births have an influence on these women setting independent households, it would appear that as long as premarital births continue to rise there will be an increase in single-female-parent households. Other scientists (Jackson, 1971, 1973) have in fact showed that a significant inverse relationship ($r = -.68$) exists between the ratio of African-American men to women and the number of female-headed households. In other words, as the ratio decreases, the number of female-headed households increases. Other researchers (Scott, 1976; Madhubuti, 1990) also concluded that the sharing of the desirable yet scarce African-American males has definitely become one recognizable family arrangement. African-American men realize that, based on the statistics, they are dying and being imprisoned at rates that are by far greater than anyone else in the United States. These same men are also being told that they are a commodity, and some of them are turning a most depressing situation around to provide a chance to exploit and use women. Why should the young African-American male not go out with two, three, four, or even more women? If the women are more than just willing to be content and willing to settle for less than a one-on-one, fully committed relationship, then why should the few available "good men" not have multiple partners?

What are called "broken homes" may in fact be polygamous-type families wherein the men are part-time members of the households, but are nevertheless emotionally, financially, and sexually integrated in the households. While "man-sharing" may have historical roots in polygamy, which is an African marriage tradition that sanctions men having more than one wife, the sharing of African-American men has been considered as a possible solution to the problems associated with the shortage of African-American men. These polygamous family units are typically formed in one of two ways. The first type involves a female-headed family combined with a second female-headed family, with the two females sharing the never-married father of their children. The second major type occurs where a legally married man and an unmarried female begin an extramarital courtship which eventually grows into a full-fledged familial relationship with children and subsequent regular visitation and financial support. Here, the consensual "wife" is often a never-married mother living independently who began as a teenage parent and for various social, interpersonal, and economic reasons became sexually involved with a married man and accepted the option of sharing him with his legal wife.

As indicated above, while the sharing of men may be a possible solution to the shortage of "good men," there are a number of problems and issues that have not been addressed, and the range of these sociocultural, interpersonal, and legal problems far exceeds the limits of this book. Be that as it may, the health implications associated with the "man-sharing" arrangement may be detrimental to the survival of the African-American race because of the emergence of HIV/AIDS in the African-American community.

It is unfortunate that the AIDS epidemic among African-Americans comes at a time when we are struggling with other important issues concerning the well-being of our cultural and ethnic identity. We as a people have faced many problems and obstacles to our survival, but HIV/AIDS is a problem that must be effectively dealt with by refuting myths about the sexuality of African-Americans as well as by accepting certain realities about sex and politics. Because these issues are so deeply woven and intertwined with racism and racial superiority, the health and economic consequences related to HIV/AIDS will be one of our most difficult problems to overcome. It should also be noted that monogamy is no guarantee against infection; the only way two people can be sure that they are disease-free is by getting tested for HIV. You cannot tell if a person is infected by looking at them, and many sexually transmitted diseases have no symptoms. In addition, like it or not, people lie about their sexual history mainly to increase their appeal. People also lie about their present monogamy and possibly their health status in order to acquire a new partner.

Although bisexual and homosexual contact between men continues to remain the most common mode of HIV/AIDS transmission among all ethnic groups, the alarming increase in the rate of HIV among heterosexual males who do not identify themselves as "gay" warrants serious attention. This fact is especially important in light of recent findings which indicate that approximately 50 percent of all male heterosexual cases are African-American. Several studies of the association between IV-drug use and the spread of HIV have shown that a larger proportion of males with AIDS were heterosexual IV-drug abusers or had a female sex partner who was an IV-drug abuser.

The omission of specific information regarding the relationship between ethnicity and high-risk sexual behavior related to HIV infection has made it difficult to determine the attitudes that African-Americans, particularly individuals engaging in risky sexual behaviors, maintain about AIDS or their attitudes about making changes in their sexual practices. As a consequence, much of our understanding of how to change the sexual practices, attitudes, and lifestyles of young African-Americans has been derived from a limited number of studies comparing African-Americans and whites. An earlier study by Seltzer and Smith (1988) supports the need for more detailed investigations of attitudes/knowledge about AIDS and condom usage among African-American groups at high risk for HIV infection. Data obtained from their large national survey indicated that while whites had greater knowledge and held less misconceptions about AIDS, significant differences between African-American and white respondents disappeared after controlling for education. African-Americans were more likely than whites to report two or more sex partners in the past year (22 percent versus 11 percent). Among white respondents, those with multiple sex partners were better able to assess their own risk compared to respondents without multiple sex partners (24 percent versus 7 percent). However, among African-Americans there was no corresponding relationship between multiple sex partnership and perceived risk for AIDS.

Although there were ethnic differences in attitudes about the use of condoms and sex within or outside monogamous relationships, the investigation was not thorough enough to provide information that is necessary for the development of effective AIDS prevention programs for African-American adults. A number of researchers have demonstrated an association between HIV seropositivity and a number of health and sexual practices. Among the risk factors most frequently identified among homosexual males and paralleled in heterosexuals are multiple sexual partners, risky sexual practices (anal intercourse, oral sex, and sex with members of high risk groups), history of sexually transmitted diseases, substance use, and lack of condom usage (Kelly and Lawrence, 1988). To the extent that these factors are prevalent in African-American adolescents and young adults, these individuals may be at potential risk for acquiring HIV infection and AIDS.

Whereas condoms have been demonstrated as a protective mechanism against HIV infection (Kelly and Lawrence, 1988; Baffi, Schroeder, Redican, and McCluskey, 1989; Goldsmith, 1987), a number of studies described elsewhere in this book document the low rate of condom use among young adults. In addition, since HIV infection is present in the sexually active population and is sexually transmitted, the likelihood of exposure should vary with the number of sexual partners encountered (Kelly and Lawrence, 1988). Given this fact, seemingly greater numbers of individuals would become involved in monogamous relationships in response to AIDS. Again, this self-protective behavior has not been demonstrated in large proportions of the adolescent/young adult community. In fact, the recent data on the prevalence of individuals involved with multiple sex partners is a bit disturbing. For example, the results of Baldwin and Baldwin's (1988b) random sample of university students revealed that the average number of sexual partners for sexually active individuals was two within the last three months. Kegeles et al. (1988) found that during the year between their follow-up study, over 40 percent of females and 69 percent of males had more than one sexual partner. All ethnicities were represented in this study. Likewise, Turner et al. (1988) found that more than 60 percent of their sample of Oxford University students had more than one partner. Twenty-eight percent of women and 27 percent of men had two or three partners, while 36 percent of women and men had more than three partners.

Other research has documented the prevalence of multiple partnerships among college students. For example, Hernandes and Smith (1990) noted that during the prior 23 weeks of their study, 56 percent of their sample had sexual relations with more than one partner. Ten percent had more than one ongoing sexual relationship. Overall there were more men (52 percent) than women (38 percent) with multiple partners, and a larger percentage of women (41 percent) than men (2 percent) with only one partner. Of the 68 sexually active students who were not serially monogamous, 80 percent had more than one partner and only 25 percent had used a condom during the previous 23 weeks.

Thomas, Gilliam, and Iwrey's (1989) survey of young African-American adults revealed that over 17 percent of men and 14 percent of women were sexually involved with more than one partner. Another study of young African-American adults indicated that 42 percent of African-American men and 18 percent of African-American women (median age 24 and 22 respectively) attending an STD clinic in Baltimore were sexually involved with multiple sex partners (Quinn, Cannon, Glasser, Groseclose, Brathwaite, Fauci, and Hook, 1990). Research surveying African-American teenage crack users indicated that multiple sexual partnerships among this population were common, with boys reporting having had more than ten sexual partners within the last year than girls (Fullilove, Fullilove, Bowser, and Gross, 1990a, 1990b).

A few studies have documented that a proportion of adolescents/ young adults also engage in risky sexual practices such as oral and anal sex. The results from one study show that 10 percent of predominantly white adolescent females engaged in oral sex, while 83 percent had practiced oral sex and 88.6 percent were the recipients of oral-genital sex. None of the subjects who practiced anal sex used condoms (Catania, Dolcini, Coasters, Kegeles, Greenblatt, Puckett, Croman, and Miller, 1989). The Jaffe, Seehaus, Wagner, and Leadbeater (1988) study of predominantly African-American and Hispanic females revealed that oral sex was practiced by 48 percent of respondents and 25 percent had engaged in anal intercourse. The practice of anal sex was significantly positively correlated with age, and there was a trend for oral sex to increase with age. Additional research has also indicated that a majority of sexually experienced males and females (85 percent) have had oral sex and 18 percent have experienced anal sex (Ishii-Kuntz, 1988). Over 5 and 10 percent of males and females respectively had engaged in anal sex among the sample of young African-American adults examined by Thomas et al. (1989).

An additional study reported a higher percentage of African-American men (11.3 percent) engaged in sex with high risk members compared to women (Quinn, Cannon, Glasser, Groseclose, Brathwaite, Fauci, and Hook, 1990).

As far as the information collected for this book goes, it was hypothesized that African-American males and females with multiple sexual partners would have a lower level of knowledge about AIDS and the use of condoms as a means of preventing the spread of AIDS. It was also hypothesized that drug usage and the prevalence of STDs would be higher among African-American males and females with multiple sexual partners. It is also hypothesized that African-American males would have more negative attitudes and emotional reactions, particularly anger, regarding the use of condoms than African-American females. Based on findings derived by Seltzer and Smith, it was also predicted that African-American males and females who are sexually involved with multiple partners would not perceive themselves to be at increased risk for contracting HIV/AIDS compared to individuals involved with a single partner.

For purposes of this study, a subject was classified as having multiple sexual partners (MSP) if he or she answered "yes" to the following question: "At the current time, I have more than one girlfriend (or boyfriend) that I have sexual relations with on a regular basis." Subjects were classified as not having a multiple sexual partner (N-MSP) if they responded "no" to the question. Of the 200 men, 94 (47 percent) reported that they were currently involved with more than one sexual partner while 106 were classified as not having multiple sexual partners. Of the African-American women who completed the study 39 (19 percent) were classified as having multiple sexual partners while 166 were classified as not having multiple sexual partners. While the percentage of males and females sexually involved with multiple partners appears to be high, these data are quite similar to the percentage of white male (52 percent) and female (33 percent) college students who are sexually involved with more than one partner (Hernandez and Smith, 1990). On average, 56 percent of the subjects who were sexually active reported having had sexual intercourse with more than one partner during the previous 23 weeks, and 35 percent of the students reported using condoms regularly during this time period.

MULTIPLE SEX PARTNERS AMONG AFRICAN-AMERICAN WOMEN

It has been suggested that one of the factors associated with the spread of HIV infections among young adults is the practice of non-monogamous sexual relationships. As indicated earlier, few studies have examined the interrelationships between sexual behavior and attitudes about the use of condoms among African-American women within monogamous and non-monogamous relationships. There is a need for systematic research with this population because African-American women with multiple sex partners may be at increased risk for HIV infections. The women in my study completed questionnaires about their attitudes and knowledge about the use of condoms and AIDS. Also included in the questionnaire were items that measured drug usage and history of sexually transmitted diseases. The results of this investigation indicated that negative attitudes about the use of condoms were significantly higher among women with multiple sex partners. However, knowledge about the transmission of AIDS was quite high among women in both groups. Women in both groups were well aware of the fact that using a condom during sex can lower the risk of getting AIDS. Nevertheless, a very low percentage of women in the MSP group (14 percent) and the N-MSP (28 percent) "always" use condoms with their partners. Finally, the prevalence of STDs and drug usage (i.e., smoking, drinking, and using crack cocaine) was higher among women in the MSP group. Specifically, the percentage of women in the MSP group with gonorrhea (7 percent), herpes (7 percent), and genital warts (10 percent) was significantly higher than the percentage of women involved with a single partner (4 percent, 1 percent, and 4 percent respectively).

The overall results from this investigation are disquieting and alarming to those of us who conduct research on the psychosocial correlates of health among young African-American adults. First of all, 19 percent of this group of well-educated African-American women were currently sexually involved with more than one male partner. Although knowledge about the spread of HIV and AIDS was generally quite high for women with and without multiple sexual partners, African-American women in the MSP group tended to have a few important misperceptions about AIDS. For example, a significantly lower percentage of the women in the MSP group knew that AIDS is not caused by the same virus that causes VD (67 percent versus 90 percent of the women in the N-MSP group) and that AIDS is not caused by bacteria (27 percent versus 57 percent of the women in the N-MSP group). A significantly lower percentage of African-American women in the MSP group knew that there is no cure for AIDS (82 percent versus 94 percent of the women in the N-MSP group) and that people with AIDS usually have other life threatening diseases as a result of AIDS (52 percent versus 80 percent of the women in the N-MSP group).

Taken together, these data indicate that African-American women with multiple sex partners may *not* perceive themselves to be at increased risk for HIV infection or worry about getting AIDS because they believe that HIV/AIDS is caused by treatable conditions such as bacteria and the same virus that causes VD. Although there are few studies with which to compare our results, we did obtain findings that are similar to Thomas et al. (1989) with regards to misperceptions that young African-American adults have about AIDS being caused by the same virus that causes STDs. In their study of 975 African-American college students, Thomas et al. reported that only 69 percent of the African-American students knew that AIDS was not caused by the same virus that causes herpes. Unfortunately, Thomas et al. did not break down their data by risk groups (e.g., multiple versus non-multiple partners) and it is not possible to determine that findings revealed in the two studies are compatible.

The findings of this inquiry which show that a lower percentage of the women in the MSP group (14 percent) always used condoms during the past year was not surprising since women in the MSP group had extremely negative attitudes about using condoms (e.g., using condoms is disgusting; would avoid using them if at all possible; men who use them are jerks) and lower intentions to use condoms. Interestingly enough, women in the MSP and N-MSP groups did not differ in their views of condoms as a satisfactory and effective form of contraception. Be this as it may, women in the MSP group report that they become intensely irritated and angry when their partner(s) refuses sex unless a condom is used or when the partner(s) makes inquiries about their previous sexual behavior. The present study provides very strong evidence that methods used to encourage condom use among young African-American adults have not been successful. These findings provide evidence that, contrary to conventional wisdom, the level of AIDS knowledge is exceptionally high among African-American women with multiple sex partners.

Overall, the pattern of these findings indicates that providing African-American women with information that focuses on changing their attitudes/perception and negative emotional responses to condoms, rather than information about how condoms lower the risk of HIV may be a way of motivating African-American women in "high-risk" groups to use condoms. More importantly, it is my belief that there are at least three reasons why African-American women with multiple partners do not always use condoms and have negative emotions and attitudes about the use of condoms. First, the male partner(s) may not think there is a risk of STD or HIV infection if the female partner does not insist on using a condom. This belief may be reinforced further as a result of the female partner becoming angry and enraged about the possibility of using condoms or when the male partner refuses sex unless a condom is used. In this case, the female partner may also feel insulted and angry because the male partner believes that having sexual intercourse with her is risky. The irony of it all is that African-American women with multiple sex partners have been treated for more STDs (gonorrhea, herpes, genital warts) and engage in more behaviors (e.g., anal intercourse, sex with prostitutes) that have been shown to be related to the spread of HIV (Turner, Miller, and Moses, 1989; Darrow, 1988). Furthermore, the strong correlations between the various STD measures (e.g., $r = .68$, $p < .001$ for syphilis and gonorrhea) clearly indicate that African-American women who have been treated for one STD have also been treated for other STDs (see Table 5.1). So in all honesty, it appears that the negative attitudes and emotional reactions about the use of condoms are not justified and may block or inhibit other purposes. In either case, the end result of the interaction between the partners possibly involves participation in sexual intercourse without the protection of condoms.

It is also possible that African-American women in the MSP group may not consider themselves to be at "high risk" for HIV. To a great extent this is true because only 17 percent of these women consider themselves at risk while 2 percent of the women in the N-MSP group believe they are at high risk for HIV. Although we do not know exactly why such a small percentage of the African-American women in the MSP group consider themselves at high risk, it is obvious that in light of their greater exposure to risk circumstances (i.e., previous treatment for STDs, unprotected anal intercourse) the perception of personal vulnerability is not too great. Perhaps this incongruity is partly related to the possibility that African-American women with multiple partners, once exposed to STDs, are more discriminating about their selection of male sexual partners and would therefore not have strong reasons to believe that they are at high risk for HIV.

It should also be mentioned that significant positive correlations were found between STDs and the respondent's acknowledgment that condoms were always used with partners over the past 12 months. These findings suggest that African-American women with histories of STDs have a higher level of perceived susceptibility which is hypothesized to be associated with decreases in risky behavior (Catania, Kegeles, and Coates, 1990), or as the current data indicate, an increase in the reported rate that condoms are always used with partners. Thus, women who have been treated for STDs may be judging their susceptibility to be exposed to HIV/AIDS to be higher than that of women who report lower risk behaviors such as lower exposure to STDs and anal intercourse. It is also possible that African-American women with histories of STDs may have a higher level of perceived vulnerability to HIV and therefore use strategies to reduce the risk (e.g., have their partner use condoms). However, our data do not support this line of reasoning because the women in the present inquiry report that they are intensely irritated and enraged when their partner refuses sex unless a condom is used. Though the answers to the questions raised by these data are beyond the scope of the present study, there is a need to investigate these concerns because those heterosexual women who engage in sexual intercourse (e.g., oral, anal, etc.) with multiple partners without condoms are placing themselves and their partners at possible risk for HIV and AIDS. For example, the results of a study published in September, 1991 in the *Journal of the American Medical Association* indicates that it is much easier for the virus to be transmitted from an infected man to an uninfected woman. In this study, which was directed by Nancy Padian of the University of California at San Francisco (Padian, Shiboski, and Jewell, 1991), the transmission of the AIDS virus was examined among a sample of 379 heterosexual couples. The results of this study revealed that there were 61 cases in which an HIV-infected man gave the virus to a woman, while there was only one case in which an infected woman gave the virus to a man. It should be noted that in this single case, the couple engaged in a number of risky sexual behaviors such as unprotected anal intercourse and swapping sex partners.

Generally speaking, women have higher odds of being infected by a man who is HIV-positive than the reverse. One of the main reasons for this is that infected semen can remain in the vagina and uterus for days. On the other hand, a man is only exposed to infected vaginal secretions during the sexual act, and unless he has cuts on his penis or genital lesions the odds of him being infected are very low.

It is also my belief that African-American women in the MSP group may not always use condoms with their partners because of personal disturbances such as diminished self-worth, profound feelings of hopelessness and loneliness, or excessive use of drugs. Although we did not obtain measures of psychosocial distress in this investigation, current research indicates that African-Americans suffer from greater exposure to life stress which is strongly related to the onset and maintenance of health problems (Johnson and Broman, 1987; Broman and Johnson, 1988; Johnson, 1990; U.S. Department of Health and Human Services, 1985). Perhaps women in the MSP group seek multiple partners as a way of helping themselves to feel accepted and loved by others or as a means of using sex to reduce the stress in their lives. On the other hand, the study did find that the use of certain drugs (cigarettes, marijuana, cocaine) was higher among women in the MSP group.

One problem with the assessment of drug use was that the measures used did not determine whether drugs were used as part of the routine of sexual intercourse. Nevertheless, the data do not show (see Table 7.2) that the use of certain drugs was significantly related to STDs, having four or more partners over the past 12 months, or attitudes about condoms. Given the reported relationship between drug use and high-risk sexual activities (Fullilove et al., 1990; Zabin, Hardy, Smith, and Hirsch, 1986; Des Jarlis, Wish, Friedman, et al., 1987; Turner, Miller, and Moses, 1989; Primm, 1990) the lack of significant associations between drug use and sexual behavior was surprising. However, as indicated earlier, we did not identify whether drug use occurred during foreplay or sexual intercourse. It is also possible that the reported association between drug use and risky sexual behaviors is restricted to populations with a higher probability of exposure to HIV/AIDS (e.g., IV-drug users).

In conclusion, the data are supportive of important interrelationships between negative attitudes about using condoms, sex with multiple partners, inconsistent use of condoms over the past 12 months, and STDs. The point to be emphasized here is that these data were obtained from a cross-sectional and non-random sample, and, as has been the case with several of the studies conducted by researchers in this area, it is difficult to determine the exact direction of causality between variables in this study. While knowledge about the transmission of AIDS was exceptionally high for African-American women with and without multiple sex partners, knowledge about AIDS (e.g., using condoms lowers the risk of HIV infection) contributed very little to understanding the sexual behavior and attitudes of women with multiple sex partners. It was also discovered that drug use was unrelated to STDs. As indicated above, the cross-sectional nature of the data makes it difficult to judge the causal direction of the findings. Nevertheless, the present investigation identifies a number of methodological problems and limitations inherent in the present investigation (and others) which makes it difficult to generalize the findings to other populations. First, the use of convenient samples of college students may limit the generalization of findings. In fact, the observed relationships between variables in this study may be stronger and more exaggerated among women from other populations (e.g., non-college bound women, alcoholic and drug abusers, women attending STD treatment clinics). In either case, the findings obtained from select samples are likely to be biased and include individuals who are more willing to be truthful about their personal behaviors. Second, the present study did not adequately assess the frequency of sexual behavior or determine which sexual partner expressed the desire to use condoms. Previous research

(Kegeles, Adler, and Irwin, 1988; Rickert, Gottlieb, and Bridges, 1989; Catania, Dolcini, Coates et al., 1989) suggests that it may be very important to measure these variables in subsequent studies because both males and females may be uncertain about the desire of their partner to use condoms.

Assessment of other factors such as communication and anger-coping styles may also be very relevant given the findings which show that women in the MSP groups react with intense anger when their partner inquires about their previous sexual behavior or refuses sex unless a condom is used. There is also a need for research to focus on the use of drugs as part of the sex routine and the impact that drug use has on the use of condoms and the engagement in behaviors that are associated with increased risk for HIV infection. It can also be argued that the description of multiple and non-multiple sex partner relationships is a bit confounded. For example, there are several types of multiple-sex-partner or non-monogamous relationships and this study examined only one type—concurrent multiple relationships with different partners. This inquiry failed to assess sequential monogamous relationships—the situation in which a woman is involved with a succession of partners, one at a time—nor did it determine the length of the multiple-partner relationships or the type of this non-monogamous arrangement. As a consequence, it is not possible to know to what extent N-MSP or MSP women were involved in sequential monogamous relationships or if the single women in the MSP group were involved with several single, older, or married men. Finally, there is a need to determine whether psychosocial factors such as loneliness and depression, diminished social support and low self-esteem contribute to our understanding of the sexual behavior of African-American women with multiple sex partners (Biglan et al., 1990). Without a comprehensive understanding of how these and other factors relate specifically to the behavior of African-American women, we will undoubtedly be fighting a losing battle to alter the spread of HIV/AIDS among African-American heterosexuals who engage in behaviors that put themselves at risk.

MULTIPLE SEX PARTNERS AMONG AFRICAN-AMERICAN MALES

As with the results for African-American women, knowledge about the transmission of AIDS was very high for African-American males in both groups. Nevertheless, males in the MSP group had significantly more negative attitudes about the use of condoms. The two groups did not differ in their intentions to use condoms, but only one-third of the males reported "always" using condoms over the previous 12 months. Interestingly enough, African-American males in the MSP group react with intense anger when condoms interfere with foreplay or sexual pleasures. In contrast, the angry reactions of African-American males in the N-MSP group are significantly more intense when their partner "jokes" about the use of condoms. A significantly larger percentage of African-American males in the MSP group had been treated for gonorrhea (28 percent versus 7 percent) and genital warts (8 percent versus 4 percent). The rates for the other STDs were approximately equal for males in both groups with 6 percent of the males in both groups being previously treated for herpes, 7 percent being treated for syphilis, and 7 percent testing positive for HIV/AIDS. Alcohol and marijuana use was significantly higher among males in the MSP group. However, despite popular belief, drug use was not related to STDs or to other sexual behaviors. This finding was consistent with those obtained from African-American females in the present inquiry. On the other hand, STDs among males were significantly associated with risky sexual behaviors. Finally, a larger percentage of African-American males in the MSP group reported having experienced anal intercourse (24 percent), sex with a prostitute (28 percent), and consider themselves to be at high risk for AIDS (25 percent).

Few studies have examined attitudes and behaviors related to sexual practices and lifestyles that promote or inhibit the spread of HIV infection among heterosexual African-American males. The current investigation unveils four major findings. First, as pointed out above, the overall level of knowledge about AIDS discovered was exceptionally high among African-American males with and without multiple sex partners. Second, African-American males with multiple sex partners had more negative attitudes about the use of condoms than African-American males without multiple sex partners. Third, a larger percentage of African-American males with multiple sex partners use alcohol and marijuana and have been treated for gonorrhea. Finally, a larger percentage of African-American males with multiple sex partners have experienced anal intercourse and sex with prostitutes.

Even though a larger percentage of African-American males with multiple sex partners consider themselves to be in a high-risk group for HIV infection, the overall percentage (25 percent) is quite low given the degree of risky sexual behavior (i.e., anal intercourse, sex with males, sex with prostitutes, lack of condom use with partners) among African-American males with multiple sex partners. This study is cross-sectional in nature and it struggles with issues of causality and adequacy of the measurement of sexual behaviors much like several of the other studies in this area (Thomas et al.,

1989; Jaffe et al., 1988; Mays and Cochran, 1988; Catania, Dolcini, Coates, Kegeles, Greenblatt, Puckett, Cormon, and Miller, 1989; Seltzer and Smith, 1988).

There appears to be a general consensus among AIDS researchers that a lack of knowledge of the primary routes of HIV transmission place African-Americans at a higher risk because they cannot appropriately identify their own susceptibility to the virus (DiClemente, Boyer, and Morales, 1988; DiClemente, Zorn, and Temoshok, 1987; Seltzer, Gilliam, and Stroman, 1988; Thomas, Gilliam, and Iwrey, 1989; Seltzer and Smith, 1988). However, results indicate that African-American men with and without multiple sex partners were highly knowledgeable regarding the transmission of AIDS and an exceptionally large percentage (93 percent) knew that condom use is an effective barrier against the virus. To a great extent these findings do not corroborate the earlier work of Thomas, Gilliam, and Iwrey (1989), who reported significantly less knowledge about AIDS among African-American college students who engage in high-risk behaviors. A possible reason for the discrepancy in findings is due to the fact that Thomas et al. (1989) did not break down their data by gender. Even though knowledge about AIDS was generally quite high among African-American males with and without multiple sex partners, African-American males in both groups have a few important misperceptions about the spread of AIDS. For example, only 58 percent of the overall sample of African-American males knew that AIDS is not caused by bacteria. Similarly, only 75 percent of the African-American males knew that people with AIDS usually have other diseases as a result of AIDS, while only 59 percent knew that the cause of AIDS is unknown. Whereas it is possible to understand how questions like the latter one may have been misunderstood, the fact that only 86 percent of the African-American males knew that AIDS is not caused by the same virus that causes VD is reason to be concerned. In other words, these findings could be taken to indicate that a subgroup of African-American males may believe that AIDS is treatable much like VD or a bacterial infection. There appears to be a need for additional education on these topics.

Another major finding uncovered by this investigation was the significant difference in the attitudes toward condom use among African-American males with and without multiple sex partners. The analyses of these data indicated that a specific cluster of items separated the two groups. These items appear to be relevant to condoms being inconvenient and interfering with foreplay and sexual pleasures. The two groups did not differ with regards to their attitudes about using condoms as a contraceptive or the belief that the use of condoms can be a highly erotic experience.

It is noteworthy that African-American males with multiple sex partners experience more intense angry reactions when condoms interfere with foreplay and sexual pleasures compared to African-American males in the N-MSP group who react with anger when their partner "jokes" about the use of condoms or insists on not using a condom during sexual intercourse. Even though African-American males with multiple sex partners endorsed more negative attitudes about using condoms, they did not differ significantly from African-American males in the N-MSP group with regards to their intentions to use condoms or their use of condoms over the previous 12 months. In fact, 34 percent of the African-American men in the MSP group and 30 percent of the African-American men in the N-MSP group indicated that they "always" used condoms with their partner over the previous 12 months. In other words, nearly 70 percent of the overall sample of African-American males indicated that they did not always use condoms with their partners. To a certain extent our findings complement earlier findings from a study by Rickert et al. (1989, 1990) where it was discovered that the majority of young women in their study would ask their partner to use condoms, but only 39 percent of the male partners had a history of purchasing condoms.

There is a strong concern among researchers that many of the problem behaviors that are associated with the spread of STDs are identical to those that are associated with the spread of HIV infections. The finding of the present inquiry shows that a significantly larger percentage of African-American males with multiple sex partners have been previously treated for gonorrhea (28 percent) compared to the N-MSP group (8 percent). More specifically, the rate for gonorrhea was three times greater among African-American males with multiple partners. In contrast, there were no significant differences between the two groups in the percentage of African-American males previously treated for the other STDs (e.g., syphilis was 7 percent for each group; herpes was 6 percent for each group; genital warts was 8 percent for the MSP and 4 percent for the N-MSP group; HIV/AIDS was 7 percent for the MSP and 6 percent for the N-MSP group). The overall percentage of STDs within the sample of African-American males was 10 percent. Comparatively speaking, this rate is a bit higher than the rate (6.8 percent) reported by Thomas et al. (1989) and it may be related to the fact that they did not present their data in a way to compare findings separately for males and females. However, these differences could be related to the fact that STDs are on the rise among young African-Americans and the higher rate obtained in 1990/91 is a mere reflection of this trend. It was also observed that, on average, 13.2 percent of the African-American males in the MSP group had been previously treated for an STD compared to 6.2 percent of the African-American males in the N-MSP group. Gonorrhea, the most prevalent STD among African-American males, was significantly correlated positive with syphilis ($r = .50$, $p < .001$), herpes ($r = .51$, $p < .001$), genital warts ($r = .54$, $p < .001$), and HIV/AIDS ($r = .56$, $p < .001$). In other words, the odds are quite high that if an African-American male has contracted one STD he has been exposed to several others.

Of most importance was the fact that each of the STDs was significantly correlated positive with HIV/AIDS and that HIV/AIDS was significantly associated with risky bisexual behaviors such as having sex with males ($r = .48$, $p < .001$), unprotected anal intercourse ($r = .46$, $p < .001$), and having four or more partners ($r = .42$, $p < .001$) in the past year. Clearly, the observed associations between STDs and risky sexual behaviors indicate that a relatively large percentage of young adult African-American heterosexual males are engaging in behaviors that are increasing their risk of being exposed to AIDS.

The results of the present inquiry also showed that a larger percentage of African-American males in the MSP group reported having experienced anal intercourse and sex with prostitutes (24 percent and 28 percent, respectively) compared to the N-MSP group (14 percent and 8 percent, respectively). While I have no previous data with which to compare these findings, I am a bit distressed by the overall pattern of these results primarily because a relatively small percentage of the African-American males in the MSP (25 percent) and the N-MSP groups (3 percent) considered themselves to be at high risk for AIDS. Even though the percentage of African-American males in the MSP group who consider themselves at high risk for AIDS is significantly higher than the percentage of males in the N-MSP group, the percentage of the males who reported that they "always" used condoms with their partners was very small for both groups (34 percent for MSP and 30 percent for N-MSP). These data are particularly distressing because of the large percentage of AIDS cases in the United States that are associated with homosexuality and presumably the practice of anal intercourse. Another reason for concern is that several of the males in both groups engage in sexual intercourse with other males (4 percent of the MSP and 10 percent of the N-MSP).

The overall pattern of the findings indicates that African-American males with multiple sex partners are engaging in sexual behaviors that are potentially placing themselves and their partners at high risk for HIV infection. However, these males do not perceive themselves to be at high risk even though they are highly knowledgeable about factors related to the spread of AIDS. The findings from this investigation are alarming and this inquiry represents a first step in understanding the interrelationships between knowledge and attitudes about AIDS and condom usage among African-American males. However, there is a possibility that subjects who participated in this study were individuals who were more willing to be truthful about revealing sensitive information about their sexual behaviors. It is also possible that the use of a non-random college sample of African-American males clearly minimizes the generalizability of these findings to other populations of African-American males. However, if the 4 to 6 percent of African-American males who attend college are the "cream of the crop," then it may very well be true that African-American males are headed for extinction. Mounting evidence suggests that a near majority of working-age African-American males between 15 and 45 years of age are alcoholics or drug abusers, are in prisons, unemployed, or suffering from some life-threatening condition.

In this study, the assessment of anal intercourse was not as thorough as it needed to be since the measure of anal intercourse did not distinguish between insertive and receptive anal intercourse. The assessment of STDs and HIV/AIDS status was derived from self-report questionnaires and the measures may not be as accurate as information derived from a medical examination. Moreover, the respondents were asked to indicate whether they have had the various STDs and not whether they "currently" have the STDs.

Because of the issues raised above, it is not possible to fully determine whether the risky sexual behavior of individuals with multiple partners preceded or followed being exposed to the STDs, drug use (alcohol and marijuana), or the development of negative attitudes about condom usage. Another major measurement problem is that of determining the full extent of the relationships, if any, of individuals who were sexually involved with multiple sex partners. It is quite possible that individuals involved with multiple partners were not emotionally invested in the relationships and that the relationships were used exclusively to satisfy sexual needs. Some individuals could have been sexually involved solely with a prostitute on a regular basis. Clearly each of these concerns will need to be considered in evaluating the impact of the investigation, but they also represent important areas for future research. As indicated earlier, there is a notable lack of solid empirical research regarding sexual practices and behaviors of African-American males or lifestyle factors that promote the spread of AIDS among African-American male heterosexuals.

For some young African-American men living in an urban environment, choosing to have and maintain a monogamous relationship often invites ridicule. Males who play (sleep) around with two and three or more partners (two- and three-timers) actually provide strong reinforcements for this behavior by complimenting one another for "scoring" and "scooping" women. To a certain extent peer pressure provides much of the support for the involvement with multiple partners. However, it is likely that since most young African-American males cannot manifest manhood through economic and political means, they attempt to do so through juggling women in meaningless relationships because it provides them with a big ego booster, a way of making them feel like a man and better about themselves.

In summary, the findings from the present inquiry clearly indicate that we have reached young African-American men intellectually. However, there appears to be no real personal investment among these men in changing behaviors to decrease the possibility of contracting HIV/AIDS. Future research needs to more carefully examine the underlying behavioral and psychological factors that are possible barriers to the development and maintenance of safe sex practices among African-American male heterosexuals. The overall pattern of the findings indicates that it is important to determine the extent of knowledge and attitudes about HIV/AIDS and condom usage from specific populations of African-American subjects. Even though several studies have shown that knowledge about HIV/AIDS status may be effective in altering risky sexual behaviors among white male homosexuals (McCusker et al., 1988; Valdiserri et al., 1988), findings from these studies are at best marginally applicable to African-American heterosexual male populations who engage in risky sexual behavior. Given these observations it would appear necessary that future research efforts be directed at gathering more systematic information about the "usual" sexual behavior of other African-American populations and determine the adequacy of their knowledge and attitudes about HIV/AIDS and the use of condoms within and outside of monogamous relationships. Furthermore, it is my belief that this information would provide a sound foundation for development and implementation of AIDS prevention programs among heterosexual African-American males.

In general, I feel that these data don't provide an adequate explanation for the existence of multiple sex partner relationships among African-American males or females. Whereas the data are very supportive of current trends which suggest that African-American males are being shared by more than one woman, the current findings do not provide any insight into the type of non-monogamous relationships in which the males and females were involved, or the duration of their involvement in the relationships. In other words, it is possible that many of the multiple partner relationships are "short-lived" and approximate "serial monogamous" relationships. Neverthelesss, approximately 50 percent of the males and 20 percent of the females were sexually involved on a regular basis with more than one partner. Perhaps these individuals are involved with multiple partners for purely sexual reasons or the usual reasons associated with a bad or failing relationship (i.e., looking for a new and better partner). On the other hand, there is good reason to believe that many of these individuals are involved with multiple sex partners because of a real shortage of "good African-American men."

CHAPTER 5

Sexually Transmitted Diseases among African-Americans

It has been estimated that more young adults are having sexual inter-course at earlier ages and in more ways than ever before in the United States. As a consequence, there has been a higher incidence of sex-ually transmitted diseases, particularly among African-Americans. The Kinsey survey, published in 1948 and 1953, showed that by the age of 20, 73 percent of the men and 20 percent of the women had reported engaging in premarital sexual intercourse (Kinsey, Pomeroy, Martin, et al., 1948; Kinsey et al., 1953). However, by 1979, the per-centage of men who engaged in premarital sexual intercourse was only slightly changed at 77 percent for whites, while 80 percent of African-American men had engaged in premarital sexual intercourse. In contrast, the number of females who reported having engaged in premarital sexual intercourse by the age of 20 has risen. For example, by 1979, 65 percent of white females and 89 percent of African-American females had engaged in premarital sexual intercourse. As indicated above, a large percentage of young adults are more sexually active today and very likely to be involved with multiple partners and/or encounter a succession of brief (i.e., serial monogamous) relationships with a large number of partners. It should be obvious that these are some of the activities that increase the chances of being exposed to sexually transmitted diseases along with a number of other practices such as extramarital sexual relationships, having sexual experiences with prostitutes, and anal intercourse, which in-crease the risk of exposure to STDs and AIDS.

KEY FACTORS RELATED TO SEXUALLY TRANSMITTED DISEASES

Extramarital sexual relationships are relevant to the STD epidemic because of the importance of multiple partners in predicting levels of risk and the potential danger of infection to a monogamous partner. In the research conducted by Kinsey, it was discovered that 50 percent of married males and 25 percent of married females had at least one episode of sex outside of marriage (Luria, Friedman, and Rose, 1987). Similar figures were revealed by Reinisch, Sanders, and Ziemba-Davis (1988), who derived their estimates from a review of six data sets. Their estimates of extramarital sexual relationships showed that 37 percent (in a range from 20 to 50 percent) of husbands have had at least one additional partner during marriage. The estimate for wives' extramarital sexual relations, based on nine studies, was 29 percent (in a range from 20 to 54 percent). Although the reasons for extramarital affairs vary and go well beyond the scope of this chapter, the major reason is likely to involve unhappiness in the marriage and the reduction of fears about accidental pregnancies that are a consequence of the wide availability of contraceptives.

Another outlet for sexual expression outside of marriage has involved sexual experiences with prostitutes. While prostitution is not as common today as it was a century ago, a rather large percentage of males have had sexual experiences with a prostitute at least once in their lives. The number of female prostitutes in contemporary American society has been estimated to be between 200,000 and 500,000, while the number of male prostitutes is estimated to be between 250,000 and 300,000 (Darrow, 1986; Lloyd, 1976). Nevertheless, very little is known about the true prevalence of prostitution or the demographic characteristics of men (and women) who patronize prostitutes.

Kinsey reported that 69 percent of males had experienced sex with a prostitute, while other researchers (Reinisch et al., 1988; Vacalis, Shoemaker, and McAlister, 1989) have reported figures that are a bit lower. For example, Reinisch et al. (1988) obtained their estimates from data gathered from four studies and they estimated that 33 percent of males (in a range from 30 to 45 percent) had experienced sex with a prostitute at least once. On the other hand, the recently completed statewide survey of a random sample of 1,637 residents 18 years of age or older found that 10 percent of the heterosexual males and 2 percent of the heterosexual females reported having sex with a prostitute. The figures for the African-American males and females who constitute the subjects for the present inquiry show that 19 percent of males and 2 percent of females report having sexual experiences with a prostitute.

It is widely believed that people visit prostitutes because they have no other opportunities for sexual intercourse. However, the most common characteristic of customers of prostitutes is that they are married (Houck, 1984). Furthermore, another survey revealed that the average age of the customer was 35 and that most had a college education with an income that averaged over $30,000 per year. What is also striking is that none of the customers were unattractive or had difficulties finding a sex partner (Adams, 1987).

As indicated earlier, very little is known about the demographic characteristics of prostitutes or the individuals who seek sexual experiences with prostitutes. In one of the few studies involving the largest number of customers, 933 (14 of whom were women), the information was obtained from files maintained by an "escort service" that was "sexual" in nature. This particular client file was confiscated as evidence by a southern urban police department. Whereas information provided by the police for the study of the demographic factors did not include the names of the clients, there was enough information to allow the investigators to outline the clients' personal characteristics and the zip codes which were used in conjunction with census data to form a social-demographic profile of the clients. What was most striking about the summary of this information was that the individuals who made the greatest use of the prostitution service resided in areas where the majority of individuals were well educated, upper-middle class, high income professionals, white, and married. The majority of the clients purchased sexual services only once and 95 percent of the clients were local persons.

In addition to extramarital sex and prostitution, homosexual behavior in males is associated with significant personal and public health problems such as increased prevalence of STDs. The data shows that the rates of infection are disproportionately greater among homosexual males than among heterosexual males for every major sexually transmittable disease (Handsfield, 1981; Williams, 1979). While several factors are believed to be related to the disproportionate increase in STDs among homosexual males, the major reason may be related to the "gay liberation" which encouraged homosexual males and females to openly express their sexuality with a larger number of partners under conditions which resulted in the sexual encounters being quite anonymous (Sandholzer, 1983; Judson, Miller, and Schaffnit, 1977). It has also been argued that the nature of specific sexual practices, such as unprotected anal intercourse, is significantly associated with HIV infection possibly because it can cause rectal trauma if attempted too quickly and without adequate lubrication.

A recent report by Judson, Penley, Robinson, et al. (1980) clearly illustrates the differences in the prevalence of STDs among heterosexual and homosexual males. This study compared the prevalence rates of most common STDs among heterosexual and homosexual males who made, respectively, 12,201 and 5,324 visits to an STD clinic over 18 months. Overall, homosexual males were significantly more likely than heterosexual males to have gonorrhea (30 percent versus 20 percent), early syphilis (1.08 percent versus 0.34 percent), and anal warts (92.9 percent versus 0.26 percent), but less likely to have non-gonococcal urethritis (NGU) (14.6 percent versus 36.4 percent), herpes genitalis (0.9 percent versus 3.7 percent), pediculosis pubis (4.3 percent versus 5.35 percent), scabies (0.42 percent versus 0.76 percent), and genital warts (1.6 percent versus 6.7 percent). It is speculated that the higher rates of gonorrhea and syphilis result from a larger average number of sexual partners, more potential sites of infection, and more hidden and asymptomatic disease.

In addition to the higher rates of STDs among homosexual males, what is most striking is that for most STDs the differences in rates for homosexual and heterosexual males remained significant when the age and race of the individuals were considered. Several studies have provided information about the prevalence of STDs among patients attending public STD clinics (Cates, 1988; Quinn et al., 1990; Rabkin, Thomas, Jaffe, and Schultz, 1987; Landrum, Beck-Sague, and Kraus, 1988; Moss and Kreiss, 1990; Rapp, 1989; Polk et al., 1987). Rates of gonorrhea, syphilis, genital herpes, trichomoniasis, nongonococcal urethritis, pediculosis pubis, and venereal warts were ascertained according to sexual preference (homosexual, heterosexual), gender, and ethnic background. In general, these studies revealed that the number of STD cases not routinely reported to most public health agencies exceeded the number of STD cases that are routinely reported. Rates of gonorrhea were higher among males than among females and higher among African-Americans than among whites. Syphilis was most common among homosexual males, regardless of their ethnic background. Trichomoniasis was three times more frequent among African-Americans than whites. Rates of nongonococcal urethritis among heterosexual males were almost twice those found among homosexual males. Whites were more likely than African-Americans to have pediculosis pubis, scabies, and venereal warts.

The best information about the prevalence of homosexuality among males and females comes from the Kinsey report (Hill, 1987; Kinsey, Pomeroy, Martin, et al., 1948). Kinsey, in his survey of over 5,000 males, found that 10 percent were more or less exclusively homosexual for at least three years between the ages of 16 and 55. Four percent of the males were exclusively homosexual throughout their lives. His survey also revealed that 2 to 6 percent of unmarried women and 1 percent of married women were exclusively homosexual between the ages of 20 and 35. Whereas the exact prevalence figures for homosexuality are beyond the scope of this section, these data

are presented to show that it is the sexual behaviors (e.g., anal intercourse) and not the label of a person as a homosexual that is associated
with the spread of sexually transmitted diseases.

RATES AND PATTERNS OF TRANSMISSION OF
SEXUALLY TRANSMITTED INFECTIONS

Approximately 5 million people are seen each year at public STD
treatment clinics throughout the United States for conditions such
as nongonococcal urethritis, gonorrhea, genital herpes, syphilis,
trichomoniasis, and genital warts. It is also estimated that a similar
number of people visit private physicians for treatment of STDs
(Berg, 1990; Division of Sexually Transmitted Diseases, 1988). With
the exception of HIV, many of the STDs have been around for ages.
However, the traditional venereal diseases have achieved prominence
during the last decade for several reasons. Cates and Toomey (1990)
recently presented an overview of the STD problems and concluded
that they have achieved prominence for the following reasons:

1. Laboratory diagnostic techniques for detecting STDs have improved.
2. The size of the population at risk for STDs increased and is more sexually
   active.
3. The composition of the STD "core" population changed in such a way that
   homosexual males are more liberal and the increased use of illicit drugs
   (such as crack cocaine) has influenced a greater number of persons to exchange sex for drugs.
4. The incidence of newer STDs increased.
5. A higher proportion of infections (e.g., hepatitis A and B viruses, cytomegalovirus) with multiple modes of transmission are being transmitted
   sexually, especially among individuals engaging in anal sex.
6. The impact of STDs on maternal and child health has become apparent.
   For example, it is estimated that the cost of pelvic infection and its sequelae
   tubal infertility and ectopic pregnancy is over 2 billion dollars annually
   in the United States.
7. The STDs have been associated with incurable fatal conditions such as
   AIDS, HIV-associated genital cancers, and chronic recurrent genital herpes.
8. International travel disseminates STDs, making them a global problem.

Syphilis

As indicated earlier in this chapter, many of the STDs have existed
in epidemic proportions for a long time before the HIV/AIDS epidemic. This is obviously more true for syphilis than most other STDs.

Figure 5.1
Primary and Secondary Syphilis Cases by Gender and Race (Blacks vs Whites) in the United States from 1981 to 1988

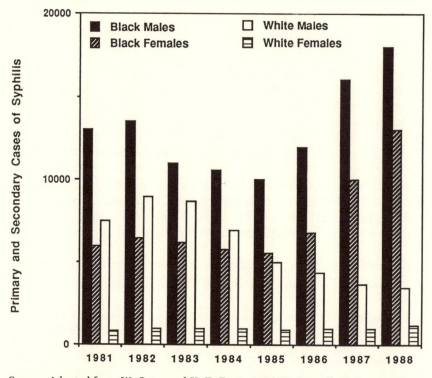

Source: Adapted from W. Cates and K. E. Toomey (1990), Sexually Transmitted Diseases, *Sexually Transmitted Diseases* 17: 1–26.

Syphilis has become more of a problem because of its association with HIV transmission and because of its escalating rate of occurrence among African-Americans and other minority heterosexuals who reside in the inner city. The number of primary and secondary cases of syphilis in the United States has declined since the introduction of penicillin in the late 1940s. In recent years, however, the trend in the rates of syphilis have been affected by homosexual behavior with a steady increase during the 1970s followed by a steady decrease in the 1980s. This most recent decline presumably reflects behavioral changes made by white homosexuals to reduce the risk of transmitting HIV and AIDS. On the other hand, the number of reported cases of infectious syphilis increased dramatically to its highest level in 40 years during the second half of the 1980s (CDC, 1988; Cates and Toomey, 1990; Fichtner, Aral, Blount, et al., 1983). As Figure 5.1 shows, this increase has occurred largely among black

(African-American) heterosexuals, particularly males. Moreover, other factors contributing to this increase include poverty (low income), residing in the inner city and the exchange of sexual services for drugs, especially crack cocaine (CDC, 1988a, 1988b, 1988c; Rolfs and Coates, 1989; Rolfs, Goldberg, and Alexander, 1988; Fullilove and Fullilove, 1989; Fullilove, et al., 1990a, 1990b). What is most startling about these data is that the reported rates for primary and secondary syphilis among African-Americans in 1980 was estimated to be 45 times the rate for whites (Moran, Aral, Jenkins, Peterman, and Alexander, 1988; CDC, 1988b) and the most current data suggest a continuation of these trends into the 1990s.

The increasing syphilis rates among African-Americans is potentially more disastrous than it appears since the increases in the number of reported cases among heterosexuals predict similar trends in congenital syphilis and because genital ulcers, associated with syphilis, are associated with HIV transmission (Pepin, Plummer, Brunham, et al., 1989). To a certain extent, there is current evidence to show substantial increases in congenital syphilis since 1984. However, a major contributor to the observed increases may be the change in surveillance definitions and the fact that serologic testing is often part of the prenatal care that is provided for poor women.

Gonorrhea

The recent gonorrhea trends in the United States show two major activities: (1) a substantial decrease in cases caused by penicillin-sensitive organisms and, (2) the continued increase in the number and variety of antibiotic-resistant strains. Like syphilis trends, a decrease in the incidence in the population of white homosexuals accounted for most of the gonorrhea decreases among men. It has been suggested that this decrease is related to the adoption of safer sexual practices (Handsfield, 1985; Judson, 1983; Schultz, Friedman, Kristal, et al., 1984; Cates and Toomey, 1990). Whereas the decline has occurred among both males and females, the rate of decrease for males has been faster, and the incidence rate for African-Americans is disproportionately higher than for whites. The most current data reveal that the incidence rate per 100,000 people of gonorrhea among African-Americans was 1,801 while the figures for whites was 54. These data translate into a rate for African-Americans that is 34 times higher than for whites (Moran et al., 1988).

Since 1980, and especially in the last four years, the incidence of beta-lactamase-producing Neisseria gonorrhoeae (PPNG) has increased dramatically. The discovery of PPNG in 1976 marked the beginning of an accelerated trend toward increased antibiotic resistance. In fact, since the emergence of PPNG, clinically significant

resistance has been found for the three most widely used classes of
drugs (penicillins, tetracyclines, and aminoglycosides-spectinomycin),
and in 1988 PPNG strains accounted for 4.4 percent of national
gonococcal morbidity (Jaffe, Biddle, Johnson, et al., 1981; Whittington
and Knapp, 1988; Cates and Toomey, 1990). In addition to the problems associated with antibiotic resistance, it has become necessary
to understand the factors associated with repeated infection due to
Neisseria gonorrhoeae. A study by Brooks, Darrow, and Day (1978)
was designed to assess the epidemiological importance of repeated
infections and to determine the variables associated with repeated
gonorrhea. This study involved a retrospective analysis of 7,347 patients seen during one year and a prospective study of a stratified,
randomly selected sample of 492 patients. The 492 retrospectively
identified repeaters constituted 6.7 percent of the clinic population,
and 29.4 percent of the cases of gonorrhea reported from the clinic.
The repeaters tended to be younger than those without repeated infection ($p < .001$), male (62 percent), African-American (82 percent), and
residents of areas of lower socioeconomic status than those who were
not repeaters ($p < .001$). Most repeaters (74 percent) had not gradu-
ated from high school. However, the repeaters did not have a significantly greater number of sex partners ($p < .05$) or greater exposure
to prostitutes than those who did not have repeated infections.

Genital Herpes

Infections with herpes virus are the main cause of genital ulcers
in the United States and account for at least ten times more cases
than syphilis (Becker, Stone, and Cates, 1986). The number of
physician-patient consultations for genital herpes increased 15-fold
between 1966 and 1987, from 30,000 to approximately 450,000, and
women aged 20 to 29 visited physicians more frequently than men
for treatment of genital herpes.

One of the most striking recent findings about the epidemiology
of genital herpes is that symptomatic infections are minimal estimates of the magnitude of the disease and its transmission (Becker,
Stone, and Cates, 1986; Guinan, Wolinsky, and Reichman, 1985;
Johnson, Nahmias, Magder, et al., 1989). For example, it is estimated
that only one-fourth of the individuals with antibodies to HSV-2 have
histories compatible with genital herpes infection, and it is estimated
that over 30 million Americans are probably infected with HSV-2.
Among African-Americans and whites, the prevalence of HSV-2 is
likely to be higher among women than men, while African-Americans
are more likely to have HSV-2 antibodies than whites (Cates and
Toomey, 1990). Another feature of HSV that is very problematic is
that in approximately three-fourths of those who are the sources of

infection, there are no genital lesions at the time of contact or any symptoms compatible with genital herpes (Mertz, Coombs, Ashley, et al., 1988; Rooney, Felser, Ostrove, et al., 1986).

Genital Human Papillomavirus (HPV) Infections

For the most part, the epidemiology of HPV infections is very similar to that of genital herpes. The major exceptions, however, are that the magnitude of symptomatic disease is approximately three times higher and the major consequence associated with HPV infection, cervical neoplasia, is more severe (Koutsky, Galloway, and Holmes, 1988; Grubb, 1986). Much like herpes, genital warts represent only a superficial symptom of HPV infection and a not-too-exact estimate (most likely an underestimate) of the magnitude of the disease. Nevertheless, by using genital warts as an index of HPV infections it has been estimated that the number of physician-patient consultations for HPV increased to nine times the number for the period between 1966 and 1987, from 179,000 to 1,860,000. As with herpes, physician visits for women outnumbered those for men and significantly more visits were reported for persons aged 20 to 29.

Chlamydia

Recent data suggest that genital infections caused by Chlamydia trachomatis are the most common bacterial sexually-transmitted syndromes in the United States today (Cates and Toomey, 1990; Thompson and Washington, 1983). Since 1972, Nongonococcal urethritis (NGU), which is a surrogate measure of Chlamydia trachomatis infections in men, surpassed gonorrhea as the most common sexually transmitted disease in the United States. In recent years, the gap has widened with patient visits to private physicians being approximately twice as common for NGU (700,000) as compared to visits for gonococcal urethritis (240,000). Approximately 2.6 million chlamydia infections occurred in women, 1.8 million in men, and .25 million in infants. In addition to its role in male infections, chlamydia plays a significant role in causing mucopurulent cervicitis, which is the female equivalent of NGU. Among nonpregnant women, Chlamydia trachomatis is a cause of acute pelvic inflammatory disease and it predisposes pregnant women to puerperal infections (Brunham, Paavonen, Stevens, et al., 1984). The group of women at highest risk of being exposed to chlamydia infections and pregnancy complications tend to be the groups at highest risk for other STDs and problematic pregnancies (e.g., unwed teenagers who reside in urban areas, African-Americans).

In 1986, a group of investigators used Neisseria gonorrhoeae as a surrogate of chlamydia and it was estimated that chlamydia caused over 4 million infections (Washington, Johnson, Sanders et al., 1988). The ratio of Chlamydia trachomatis to Neisseria gonorrhoeae infection was found to be significantly influenced by race, pregnancy status, choice of contraceptives, proportion of infections without symptoms, and sexual preference. In other words, substantially higher chlamydia to gonorrhea ratios were present among whites, pregnant women, oral contraceptive users, and asymptomatic individuals. Furthermore, compared with gonorrhea, efforts to control chlamydia have been hampered by difficulties in diagnosis and treatment (Schachter, 1989).

A number of studies have documented the prevalence of STDs in the adolescent/young adult population, wherein an estimated 2.5 million individuals per year acquire an STD (MacDonald, Wells, Fisher, Warren, King, Doherty, and Bowie, 1990; Gibson, Hornung, Alexander, Lee, Potts, and Nahmias, 1988). As indicated earlier in this chapter, the impact of STDs on minority populations, particularly African-Americans, is tremendous, with the reported rates being well over 30 times the rates for whites. A recent report of the occurrence of herpes among college students (Gibson et al., 1988) revealed that over 56 percent of African-American students with herpes simplex virus type-1 had a history of other STDs, compared to 36 percent for white students. In another study of African-American women attending an STD clinic, 76 percent reported having at least one prior STD and over one-third had attended the clinic the previous year for treatment of an STD. In another study of African-American men and women (median age 23) attending an STD clinic, over 60 percent of the men and 50 percent of the women reported having a prior STD, with gonorrhea being cited most often.

STD HISTORY, ATTITUDES, AND SEXUAL BEHAVIOR
FOR THE CURRENT SAMPLE

Among the sample of African-American college females, 12.2 percent reported having a prior STD, while approximately twice as many males (22 percent) as females reported having a prior STD. Of the women with a prior STD, gonorrhea was the most prevalent STD with 76 percent of the women reporting a history of gonorrhea. The data for males was quite similar with 65 percent of the African-American college males with a prior STD reporting a history of gonorrhea. Table 5.1 shows the prevalence of STDs among African-American male and female college students with a history of a prior STD.

A larger percentage of females than males reported a history of

Table 5.1
Prevalence of Sexually Transmitted Diseases (STDs) among African-American College Students with a History of STDs

	Females	Males
Gonorrhea	76%	65%
Syphilis	30%	17%
Herpes	25%	16%
Genital warts	27%	42%
HIV/AIDS	29%	24%

syphilis (30 percent versus 17 percent) and herpes (25 percent versus 16 percent), while a larger percentage of males (42 percent) reported having a history of genital warts than females (27 percent). Roughly one-fourth of the males (29 percent) and females (24 percent) with a prior STD reported testing positive for HIV/AIDS. To a large extent, the information derived from the current data complements findings obtained from other studies which show females visiting physicians and STD clinics more often than males for treatment of syphilis and herpes. These data also firmly indicate that a prior history of STDs is present among approximately one-fourth of African-American young adults who reported testing positive for HIV/AIDS.

Knowledge about the transmission of AIDS was uniformly quite high for both males and females with and without a previous history of STDs. No significant differences were observed in the average AIDS knowledge questionnaire scores for females with (23.2 + 5.7) and without (24.5 + 2.6) a prior STD. However, among males, the average AIDS knowledge questionnaire score was lower for those with a prior STD (20.9 + 8.7) compared to those without a prior STD (22.7 + 5.6). Overall, the data regarding AIDS knowledge are consistent with earlier information presented in Chapter 3 which did not reveal a significant association between AIDS knowledge and risky sexual behaviors.

A significantly larger percentage of both males and females with prior STDs reported engaging in oral sex, anal sex, sex with prostitutes, and having had four or more partners in the previous 12 months. Each of these comparisons were examined with a chi-square analysis which revealed that the differences were significant at the $p < .001$ probability level (see Table 5.2). Individuals with and without a previous STD did not differ in their use of condoms. However, a signifi-

Table 5.2
Sexual Behaviors and Attitudes of African-American Males and Females with and without a History of STDs

Behavior/Attitudes	Females -STD	Females +STD	Males -STD	Males +STD	Chi-Square
Oral sex	46%	83%	33%	65%	28.55***
Anal sex	12%	44%	7%	44%	40.46***
Sex with prostitute	9%	12%	0%	17%	82.75***
Four or more partners in past 12 months	47%	71%	17%	28%	45.79***
Always use condoms	34%	34%	23%	41%	4.88
Condoms not necessary if you love your partner	16%	47%	15%	33%	17.96***
Consider self at high risk for AIDS	10%	34%	4%	17%	27.45***
Smoking[a]	18%	31%	17%	31%	8.93
Drinking[a]	73%	76%	75%	75%	1.70
Marijuana[a]	12%	27%	22%	45%	22.01***
Crack/cocaine[a]	4%	15%	2%	0%	26.64***

***$p < .001$
[a]Current and ex-users.

cantly larger percentage of both males and females with prior STDs reported that condoms are not necessary if you love your partner and considered themselves at high risk for HIV/AIDS. The groups were not differentiated by cigarette smoking or alcohol use, while marijauna was used by a significantly larger number of both males and females with prior STDs. Crack and cocaine were used by a significantly larger number of African-American females with prior STDs, whereas this was not true for males.

The overall pattern of the findings presented in Tables 5.1 and 5.2 clearly and strongly indicates that the odds are quite high that if an African-American young adult has been exposed to one STD, he or she has been exposed to several other STDs. Having a history of STD infections appears to be significantly related to HIV/AIDS infections for both males and females. While it is not possible to examine the causal order or the exact reasons for the association between HIV/AIDS and STD infections, these data strongly suggest that STDs are co-factors for HIV/AIDS among African-American college students. The sexual behaviors and attitudes of those students with histories of STD infections should be described as being nothing less than "risky." In addition to being infected with HIV/AIDS, individuals with STD infections engage in anal intercourse, have sex with prostitutes, have brief relationships with a large number of partners (i.e., four or more partners in the past 12 months), and yet slightly more than one-third of this group reported that they "always" use condoms with their partners. The profile of drug use among individuals with previous STD infections could be interpreted as suggesting that drug use before or during sex contributes to risky sexual behaviors by lowering inhibitions. As with the association between HIV/AIDS infections and STD infections, it is not possible to determine the causal direction for the associations between the risky sexual behaviors/attitudes and STD infections. However, it is my belief that the pendulum swings from the direction in which risky sexual behaviors are the cause of STD infections.

CHAPTER 6

Individuals Who Always Use Condoms: Their Attitudes, Beliefs, and Sexual Behaviors

In this day and age, making love using a condom is one of the few ways to have safe sexual intercourse. Several studies have indicated that latex condoms provide an effective barrier to HIV transmission and that the virus becomes partially inactivated inside the condom (Feldblum and Fortney, 1988; Van de Perre, Jacobs, and Sprecher-Goldberger, 1987). Whereas it is the male who wears the condom during sex, the attitudes of both partners will have an effect on whether condoms will or will not be used during sexual intercourse. The use of condoms offers reasonable protection against being exposed to STDs and HIV/AIDS, but some people believe that they hamper sex, reduce pleasure during sex, and reduce sexual spontaneity. Because condoms are inexpensive, easy to obtain, and can be used as a contraceptive, there is a strong need to determine the attitudes and behaviors that are present among individuals who use condoms all the time and those individuals who do not use them and who do not intend to use them.

Before advancing to the information that I collected on this topic, I want to review a few important recent studies that have examined attitudes about condoms. In a study of potential influences of condom use among 305 single (95 percent) undergraduate men at Virginia Tech during 1986, researchers found that there were no significant differences regarding attitudes about condoms between those men who reported using condoms to prevent STDs and those who used condoms as a contraceptive device. Specifically, of the males who reported that they had used condoms in the past, 12 percent said they did so to prevent STDs while 75 percent said they did so to prevent an accidental pregnancy. The number of partners the men had sexual intercourse with over the previous two months was also determined. Of the 305 males, 67 percent reported having at least one sexual partner while 19 percent reported having had sexual intercourse with 2 to 3 partners over the previous two months. Approximately 4 percent of the males reported having had four or more partners within the past two months. When subjects in this study were asked if they intended to use a condom within the next month, 50 percent responded "no" even though the overall attitude toward condoms was neither positive nor negative in this sample. Those who intended to use condoms, however, were more likely to report positive experiences and attitudes toward condoms.

Although 83 percent of the respondents stated that they would be willing to use a condom if their partner suggested the use of one, many of these men stated they would try to avoid using condoms if at all possible. Open-ended responses about condoms suggest that many men who expressed negative views about condoms were still willing to use them. Consequently, these researchers emphasize that programs should be developed to encourage female partners to initiate condom use and to encourage the female partner to use condoms in romantic and erotic ways (Baffi, Schroeder, Redican, and McCluskey, 1989).

Since negative attitudes may mediate lack of condom compliance, Tanner and Pollack (1988) examined whether or not erotic instructions presented with condoms would lead to more positive attitudes toward condoms in 36 heterosexual couples attending the University of Georgia. To qualify in this study, participants had to currently be involved in an ongoing monogamous relationship, of legal age, and using oral contraceptives. Participants were classified into three groups. One group received condoms with erotic instructions, one group received condoms alone, and a control group received neither condoms nor instructions. All groups were given a pretest regarding their attitudes toward condoms. Results indicated that the only group whose attitudes became more positive was the condom and erotic instructions group. In the journals these groups were requested to keep, the couples in the erotic instruction-condom group reported increased pleasure associated with condom use while those in the noninstruction-condom group reported more often that their sexual enjoyment decreased while using condoms. In general, these significant relationships were consistent for both males and females.

Researchers who investigated other predictors of condom use hypothesized that decreasing the number of sexual partners and increasing condom use would be associated with a number of variables. These factors include good sexual communication skills, social norms that support safe sex, feelings of susceptibility to HIV, believing one can perform behaviors that will avoid HIV infection, having positive attitudes toward safe sex, and being somewhat anxious about the threat of HIV. These investigators also hypothesized that less egocentric individuals would have fewer partners and use condoms more often. The participants in this study consisted of 114 adolescent females, ages 12 to 18, who were attending a family planning clinic in California. The majority of the adolescents were white (92 percent) while 4 percent were Hispanic and the remaining 4 percent consisted of a range of other ethnic groups. A large percentage of the females reported having experienced vaginal (97 percent), oral (86 percent), and anal (10 percent) intercourse. Of the adolescent females who were sexually active, 47 percent reported that they had used condoms with their primary sex partner only about 25 percent of the times they had intercourse. None of the subjects who were practicing anal intercourse reported using condoms.

Contrary to their hypotheses, the results of this study of adolescent females indicated that only greater enjoyment of condoms and greater willingness to request partners to use condoms were associated with frequent condom use (Catania, Dolcini, Coates, Kegeles, Greenblatt, Puckett, Corman, and Miller, 1989). While condom use was not significantly related to the number of sex partners, having more than one partner was associated with feeling susceptible to HIV, having poorer sexual communication with the primary and prospective partners, and feeling greater peer acceptance for being sexually active.

In their predominantly white sample of male (55 percent) and female (45 percent) undergraduates, Hernandes and Smith (1990) found 73 percent of their 288 participants reported using a condom during the previous 23 weeks. However, only 35 percent of the undergraduates used condoms regularly. Of those sexually active students who were not monogamous (i.e., those involved with multiple partners) only 25 percent had used a condom during the previous 23 weeks, although 80 percent of these individuals had more than one sex partner. This finding is disturbing given that having an increased number of partners coupled with the lack of condom use increases the risk for HIV infection and AIDS. Furthermore, these observations become a bit more disturbing when one considers the fact that 35 percent of the males and 7 percent of the females reported that they used alcohol or drugs to the extent that they were impaired one or more times on a date per month. The level of these impairments involved not being capable of driving an automobile, not being cautious about the choice of a sex partner, using a condom during intercourse, and participating in risky sexual behaviors (e.g., unprotected anal intercourse).

Given that the samples used in the aforementioned studies consisted primarily of white subjects, and because the data which did include information derived from African-Americans were not analyzed with regard to ethnic differences, it is uncertain as to whether results are generalizable to African-American youth and young adults. In the 1979 National Survey of Young Men, African-American males reported significantly lower rates of contraceptive use at both their first and most recent intercourse (58 percent of African-American males versus 67 percent of non-African-American males) than did non-African-Americans (Pleck, Stonenstein, and Swain, 1988; Pleck, 1989). Regarding condom use, 13.2 percent of African-American males and 21.6 percent of non-African-American males used a condom during their first intercourse. However, African-American males were more likely to use condoms during their most recent sexual intercourse (20 percent versus 17 percent).

With regard to condom compliance, a study using male and female juvenile delinquents representing a number of ethnic groups (white, African-American, Hispanic, Native American, Asian), documents the lack of condom use among adolescents. Melchert and Burnett (1990) found that birth control was not used reliably among study participants, and even when used, oral contraceptives were the most widely employed method. The sample consisted of 212 adolescents between the ages of 12 and 20 with 64 percent of the sample consisting of males and 36 percent females. In this study there was a significant positive relationship between the age at the time of the first intercourse and the reported use of birth control. However, there was no significant relationship between having accurate knowledge about sexual issues and the reported use of birth control. Only 22 percent of the participants reported using condoms.

A study of 660 inner-city African-American adolescents further revealed that although 80 percent reported ever using a contraceptive during intercourse, only 60 percent had used contraceptives during their last intercourse and of those, only 41 percent used barrier methods (i.e., condoms). An unusually large percentage of this male adolescent sample believed that condoms are a very good method of contraception. Furthermore, 17 percent reported that contraception is the responsibility of the male, while 70 percent believed that contraception is the responsibility of the female. These results confirm the necessity to explore the inconsistency and low degree of condom compliance among African-American adolescents and young adults (Clark, Zabin, and Hardy, 1984). Given the low percentage of African-American males who believe that contraception is their responsibility, it would appear that it is necessary to develop procedures to change the attitudes that they have about contraception. There is also a need to encourage females to take responsibility for contraception because of the large number of males who believe that it is the responsibility of the woman.

Additional research regarding condoms revealed that although 74 percent of a sample of 50 African-American and 49 white adolescent females (ages 12 to 19) were aware that condoms or abstinence were the most effective protection against STDs, including AIDS, only 17 percent reported buying condoms, and 39 percent reported that their male partner bought condoms. Even though a substantial percentage (62 percent) stated AIDS had influenced their sexual behavior, only 10 percent reported using condoms to reduce the risk of AIDS and 90 percent stated that they would ask partners to use a condom. Having had an STD or unwanted pregnancy did not effect the number of females who reported using condoms or the frequency of condom use. There were no ethnic differences related to condom purchase or use, but African-American participants reported that their partners bought condoms 39 percent of the time as compared to white participants whose partners purchased condoms 16 percent of the time. Consistent with prior findings, condom purchase and use was not related to AIDS knowledge. In addition, condom purchase and use was not correlated with willingness to discuss contraceptives with one's partner or behavioral risk factors (Rickert, Jay, Gottlieb, and Bridges, 1989).

In a study of 341 patients (162 males and 179 females) attending an STD clinic, with 54 percent of the men and 50 percent of the women being either African-American or Hispanic, nearly all participants reported using a condom in the past. However, 25 percent stated they had used a condom during their last intercourse. Among the men, the likelihood of condom use during their last intercourse was lower for those who reported they had used alcohol or other drugs at the time of their last intercourse, who reported they would not use a condom if they were "in love" with their partners, who stated they experienced difficulty in communicating with their partners about condoms, and who said that their partners did not want to use condoms. Among women, condom use during the last coitus was lower for those who were African-American, who reported condoms decreased pleasure, who reported they would not use a condom if they were "in love," and who reported that their partners were unwilling to use condoms (CDC, 1990b). Overall, the findings revealed no significant relationship between condom use and STD history, age, income, education, number of sex partners, knowledge about AIDS, perceived risk for HIV/AIDS infection, peer endorsement of condoms, acquaintance with an AIDS victim, or engaging in vaginal or anal intercourse.

Regardless of the factors presented above, condom use was lowest among females, blacks in particular, who reported that their partner did not want to use condoms and who believed that condoms reduced sexual pleasure. Other factors related to the low use of condoms included being involved with a steady partner. Although these findings may have limited generalizability with regard to samples that were not gathered from respondents attending STD clinics, the findings are important because the majority of the respondents who took part in this study (192 out of 341) had previously been treated for an STD. The remaining 149 individuals were newly diagnosed cases.

AFRICAN-AMERICAN MALES WHO ALWAYS USE CONDOMS

As indicated throughout this chapter, numerous studies have shown that condoms are not consistently used among individuals at risk for AIDS (Catania, Dolcini, Coates, Kegeles, Greenblatt, Puckett, Corman, and Miller, 1989; Clark, Zabin, and Hardy, 1984; Kegeles, Adler, and Irwin, 1988; Rickert, Jay, Gottlieb, and Bridges, 1989). Nevertheless, very little research has focused on the variability of condom use within the African-American male population. The major aim of most investigations of attitudes about the use of condoms has been to compare African-American and other ethnic groups with white samples, or to use the results obtained from white samples to make generalizations about the behavior and attitudes of African-Americans (Kegeles et al., 1988; DiClemente, Boyer, and Morales, 1988; Seltzer and Smith, 1988). For example, an important study that addressed changes in condom use among homosexual men in San Francisco over the period from 1984 to 1987 had a sample that was 89 percent white (Catania, Coates, Stall, et al., 1991). The investigators used data obtained from two longitudinal surveys of gay men to examine for cohort and attrition bias (i.e., instances in which repeated interviews of the same individual may produce behavioral changes that would not have occurred otherwise) effects on repeated changes in condom use by gay men and to investigate predictors of condom use.

The results of this investigation revealed that there were substantial increases in condom use, and that these changes were unrelated to attrition and cohort bias. In terms of predictors of condom use, gay men who always used condoms had higher levels of social support from informal sources of help, had more positive expectations that condom use would have positive interpersonal and personal consequences, and were more likely to be HIV positive than men who used condoms occasionally or never. This study is important because the results have several implications for AIDS prevention among gay men. In general, intervention programs that focus on social support, health, sexual pleasure, self-worth, and relationship issues are not the most likely to show a wide range of effectiveness in changing condom use. To effectively address interpersonal issues that focus on condom use, it may be necessary to explore the meanings that condom use has for the partners. For example, being asked to use a condom may be perceived as indicating a lack of trust or suggesting that the partner has been unfaithful. The findings also suggest that the use of condoms is influenced by the erotic/pleasure dimension as well as a high level of positive support for changing sexual risk behaviors. Perhaps the process of building support networks that facilitate safe sex practices may be influenced by programs that attempt to change community norms (Catania, Coates, Kegeles, Ekstrand, Guydish, and Bye, 1989; Catania, Kegeles, and Coates, 1990; Coates, 1990; Coates, Stall, Catania, and Kegeles, 1988) or provide direct assistance in building informal support groups around the topic of safe sex (Fisher, 1988; Kelley and St. Lawrence, 1988). While there are undoubtedly other important predictors of condom use (e.g., assertiveness skills, modification of the social processes that lead to sex, increasing the presexual dating period), it is startling that a study of this importance does not even discuss the possibility that the ethnic background of men may limit the generalization of their findings.

There is a strong need to know the extent to which similar beliefs and attitudes about condoms are shared by different ethnic groups. However, it is my belief that information about the variability of condom usage within samples of African-American males will provide the most relevant information for developing effective strategies for modifying negative attitudes about the use of condoms.

The task of understanding the behaviors and attitudes related to condom usage among African-American males is extremely important because of the high incidence of sexually transmitted diseases among members of this ethnic group (Clark et al., 1984; CDC, 1989a, 1989b). Therefore, this section of the chapter will cover three objectives. The first is to determine the attitudes and knowledge about condom usage among a subgroup of young African-American adult males who report that they "always use condoms with their partner(s)." A second objective is to determine whether attitudes and knowledge about condoms differ among two groups of African-American males who do not use condoms but vary in their intentions (low versus high) to use condoms. Third, the present inquiry will determine whether knowledge about AIDS, drug use, angry reactions related to use (or lack of use) of condoms, STDs, and "risky" sexual behaviors (e.g., anal intercourse, sex with prostitutes) varies with the steady use of condoms.

The rationale for testing these relationships is guided by the fact

Table 6.1
Sexual Behaviors and Attitudes of Black Men Who Vary in Their Intentions to Use Condoms

Variables	Steady Users		Low Intenders		High Intenders		F-Tests
	Mean	SD	Mean	SD	Mean	SD	
AIDS knowledge	22.3	6.9	22.3	5.3	21.6	6.6	.16
Condom attitudes	32.5	6.7	24.6	6.7	31.5	5.3	3.54***
Contraceptive	16.3	4.5	14.4	4.3	15.4	2.9	1.75
Inconvenient	7.2	3.5	11.4	3.9	8.6	2.5	12.52***
Excites	12.2	3.9	11.3	2.6	11.1	2.6	1.07
Interrupts	14.7	6.2	20.7	5.2	17.4	4.8	9.44***
Acceptable	18.3	4.8	13.4	2.7	17.2	2.1	20.59***
Angry reactions	30.0	10.6	29.8	8.2	26.8	9.9	1.41
Smoking	1.3	1.0	1.1	.5	1.9	1.7	4.35**
Drinking	2.6	1.2	3.1	1.6	2.9	1.4	.91
Marijuana	1.1	.4	1.9	1.9	1.6	1.6	2.23
Crack	1.0	.3	1.5	1.7	1.2	1.1	.88
Cocaine	1.0	.3	1.5	1.7	1.3	1.1	.79

Variables	Steady Users	Low Intenders	High Intenders	Chi-Square
Anal sex	4%	37%	17%	10.21**
Sex with males	4%	10%	7%	.89
Sex with prostitute	11%	42%	17%	9.42**
Gonorrhea	7%	37%	15%	8.48**
Syphilis	7%	16%	6%	7.33*
Herpes	7%	16%	0%	7.84*
Genital warts	4%	16%	4%	4.63#
HIV/AIDS	15%	6%	7%	1.64
Consider self at high risk	23%	11%	22%	1.64

#$p < .10$; *$p < .05$; **$p < .01$; ***$p < .001$.

that my previous analyses of these data show that roughly one-third of the sample of 150 African-American males reported that they "always" use condoms with their partner (Johnson, Gant, Jackson, Gilbert, and Willis, 1991c; Johnson, Gant, Hinkle, and Gilbert, 1992). This relationship held constant for African-American males who were sexually involved with multiple partners as well as those involved with a single partner. This inquiry was also guided by my previous research which shows that African-American males with multiple partners experience more intense angry reactions when condoms interfere with foreplay and sexual pleasure. Alternately, African-American males with a single partner react with anger when their partner "jokes" about the use of condoms or when the partner insists on not using a condom during sexual intercourse (Johnson et al., 1991c; Johnson, Gant, Hinkle, and Gilbert, 1992). The overall pattern of these findings from previous research clearly suggests that negative emotional reactions, particularly anger, may play an important role in the negotiation of safe sex practices and the steady use of condoms.

For purposes of this inquiry, a subject was classified as a Steady User of condoms if they responded "true" to the following statement: "Over the past 12 months my partner and I always used condoms when we had sexual intercourse." Subjects who indicated that they did not use condoms were further divided into two groups based on their response to a statement about their intentions to use condoms ("I intend to try condoms"). Subjects who indicated that they "agree" or "strongly agree" with the statement were considered to have High Intentions to use condoms while subjects who indicated "strongly disagree" or "disagree" were considered to have Low Intentions to use condoms. African-American males who reported that they were undecided ($n = 44$) were not considered in any analyses. Of the 106 men, 27 (26 percent) were classified as Steady Users of condoms, 31 (29 percent) were classified as Low Intenders, and 48 (45 percent) were classified as High Intenders.

The chi-square analyses comparing the demographic variables of age, education, and marital status across all three groups were not significant. Results of the comparison of the three groups indicated that knowledge about AIDS was exceptionally high for African-American males in all three groups (see Table 6.1). African-American males with low intentions to use condoms reported significantly more negative attitudes about the use of condoms (e.g., using condoms is disgusting) and reacted with more intense anger when they were asked by their partner about previous sexual contacts, when a partner refused to have sex without a condom, or when they perceived condoms as interfering with foreplay and sexual pleasure. A significantly larger percentage of Low Intenders were treated for gonorrhea, syphilis, herpes, and genital warts than males in the other groups. Drug use did not differentiate the three groups, although marijuana was used more often by males in the Low Intenders group. Finally, a larger percentage of African-American males in the Low Intenders group reported experiences with anal intercourse and sex with a prostitute, but considered themselves at lower risk for AIDS than their High Intender or Steady Use counterparts.

Undoubtedly, the use of condoms can be an effective means of preventing the spread of STDs, and they appear to offer reasonable protection against exposure to HIV. Whereas bisexual and homosexual contact between males, and needle-sharing behavior of IV-drug users remain the chief modes of transmission, there has been an alarming increase in the incidence of HIV and other STDs among African-American male heterosexuals (CDC, 1987, 1988b, 1989a, 1989b; Aral, Cates, and Jenkins, 1985; Fichtner, Aral, Blount et al., 1983; Goldsmith, 1988; Judson, Penley, Robinson, et al., 1980). As indicated earlier, there is a notable lack of research regarding lifestyle factors, attitudes, and sexual behaviors related to the initiation and maintenance of safe sex practices among African-American males (Weinstein, Goodjoin, Crayton, and Lawson, 1988). Given this fact, there is an obvious and long overdue need to closely investigate these factors among various populations of African-American males.

SUMMARY AND DISCUSSION OF THE FINDINGS FOR MALES

This inquiry revealed several important factors that may help to explain why such a low percentage of young adult African-American males use condoms with their partners. We also identified some important factors that may explain why certain African-American male adults "always" use condoms with their partners. First of all, it was discovered that there were no significant differences in the knowledge about AIDS among African-American males as a function of the extent to which they use condoms. This finding is similar to reports (Johnson et al., 1991c) which revealed that there were no substantial differences in the range of AIDS knowledge among African-American males with and without multiple sexual partners. As with African-American males with multiple sexual partners, African-American males who do not use condoms are well aware of AIDS, how it is transmitted, and the great majority know that using condoms is an effective means of reducing the chances of being exposed to HIV infection. What remains a big puzzle is why roughly two-thirds of this sample of young, well-educated, African-American males do not use condoms with their partners. Obviously, as with our sample of males with multiple sexual partners, knowledge about AIDS is not an important part of the answer.

Second, while the three groups did not differ significantly on AIDS knowledge, they did differ with regard to their attitudes and emotional reactions associated with the use of condoms. Attitudes about using condoms as contraceptives were not different for males in the three groups. A striking finding was that the attitudes about the use of condoms were unpredictably similar for African-American males who always use condoms (Steady Users) and males with high intentions to use condoms (High Intenders). In fact, the only area where the two groups differed significantly was on their attitudes about the extent that condoms are uncomfortable or interrupt sex; African-American males in the High Intenders group had more negative attitudes about this issue. Furthermore, the overall pattern of these findings shows that African-American males in the Steady User and High Intenders groups differed significantly from African-American males in the Low Intenders group in their emotional reactions about condoms. In other words, African-American males with low intentions to use condoms were more likely to perceive condoms as inconvenient or unacceptable, would avoid using them if at all possible, and would voice strong objections if their partner suggested using condoms. Unfortunately, the cross-sectional nature of these data do not permit me to determine whether the factors that discriminate Steady Users from High Intenders are predictive of the initiation and maintenance of condom use.

The third major finding revealed in this inquiry involved the angry reaction associated with the use of condoms. There were very few significant differences in the angry reaction of African-American males in the Steady User and High Intenders groups. In fact, the only item that differentiated the two groups was the intensity of anger elicited when the partner jokes about the use of condoms. African-American males in the Steady User group reacted with greater anger. It was also observed that African-American males with low intentions to use condoms react with more intense anger to a number of important situations such as (a) when condoms interrupt foreplay, (b) when condoms interfere with sexual pleasure, (c) when partner refuses to have sex unless a condom is used, and (d) when you think that your partner will reject you if your partner asks about previous sexual behavior. These findings suggest that condoms may not be used by African-American males because the males possibly use their intense angry reactions to motivate their partner(s) to have unprotected intercourse. In other words, it is conceivable that partner(s) of African-American males in the Low Intenders group would rather have unprotected sexual intercourse and not engage in behaviors that may intensify the angry reactions of their partner, or result in arguments, fights, and/or rejection by the partner. It was also discovered that African-American males with low intentions to use condoms react with less intense anger to a number of situations than do African-American males in the Steady User and High Intenders groups. For example, African-American males in the Low Intenders group reported being less irritated when their partner (a) insists on not using a condom, or (b) jokes about the use of condoms.

It is obvious that African-American males who do not use condoms could care less about using condoms and they are very much at ease with partners who would rather have unprotected sexual intercourse. It is my belief that it will be important for future work to examine more closely the role of negative emotions in the negotiation of safe sex practices among groups who are at high risk for AIDS (e.g., multiple sexual partners, persons with histories of STDs, and persons who are HIV positive).

This inquiry did not observe that drug use was significantly different among African-American males in the three groups. The only variable that clearly differentiated the three groups was cigarette smoking. Overall the pattern of the findings showed that African-American males with high intentions to use condoms smoke more often than African-American males in the Steady User and Low Intenders groups. Even though the analysis of the main group effect was insignificant for the other drug variables, subsequent comparisons were conducted. The most striking discovery was that marijuana was used more often by African-American males with low intentions to use condoms. However, given the nature of the measure of marijuana use, it was not possible to determine whether marijuana use was associated with sexual intercourse and/or the failure to use condoms during sex. There is an obvious need for future work to focus on these latter questions as they also pertain to the use of other drugs during sexual intercourse.

Another important finding uncovered in this inquiry pertains to the previous treatment for STDs among African-American males in the three groups. The data show that a significantly larger percentage of African-American males in the Low Intenders group have been treated for gonorrhea, syphilis, herpes, and genital warts. These data are consistent with reports by others (Fichtner et al., 1983; Darrow, 1976; Moss and Kreiss, 1990; Moran, Aral, Jenkins, Peterman, and Alexander, 1988) which show increases in the number of African-American males being treated for STDs.

The results also reveal that a significantly greater percentage of African-American males in the Low Intenders group also report experiencing anal intercourse and having sex with prostitutes. There is also an interesting but insignificant trend for African-American males in the Low Intenders group to report sex with males more so than the Steady Use or High Intenders groups. Whereas these findings are cause enough for concern, the data also show that there is a tendency for African-American males in the Low Intenders group to not perceive themselves as being at increased risk for being exposed to AIDS. It will be important for future research to determine what factors mediate the relationship (or lack thereof) between perceived risk and risky sexual behaviors among African-American males. It is my belief that results from these types of studies will provide information necessary to motivate African-American males to adopt safe sex practices.

Given the significant negative attitudes that African-American males have about the use of condoms, strategies to reduce exposure to STDs and AIDS should focus on other behaviors that lower the risk of contracting AIDS. For example, we know very little about partner choice or whether the African-American males who do not use condoms are ineffective in negotiating safe sex practices with their partners. There is also a strong need for future research in this area to be prospective in nature so that problems of causality are minimized.

In summary, the findings of this inquiry reveal that knowledge about AIDS is exceptionally high among African-American males who do not use condoms. African-American males with low intentions to use condoms perceive condoms as inconvenient or unacceptable, would avoid them if at all possible, and would voice strong objections when their partner wants to use condoms. Males with low intentions to use condoms also react with intense anger when condoms interfere with foreplay or sexual pleasure and when their partner refuses to have sex without a condom. Finally, African-American males with low intentions to use condoms smoke marijuana more often, a large percentage have been treated for STDs, experienced anal intercourse, and had sex with prostitutes. In contrast, they do not perceive themselves to be the kind of person to be exposed to AIDS. It appears that very few factors discriminate between African-American males with high intentions to use condoms and African-American males in the Steady User group. African-American males in the High Intenders group have more negative attitudes regarding the discomfort of condoms and the extent to which condoms interrupt sex. Males with high intentions to use condoms also smoke cigarettes more often than males in the other groups. The pattern of findings suggests that different attitudes and behaviors should be targeted for intervention efforts among young, African-American, adult males who vary in their use of, and their intentions to use condoms.

AFRICAN-AMERICAN FEMALES WHO ALWAYS USE CONDOMS

Human immunodeficiency virus (HIV), the precursor of AIDS, is spreading at an alarming rate within the African-American community, and it is women who comprise the fastest growing AIDS risk group (Mays and Cochran, 1988). Nationwide, over 100,000 women are infected with the AIDS virus. Within this group, 53 percent are

African-American and 16 percent are Hispanic (CDC, 1991a; Thomas, et al., 1989). It has been found that one of the primary modes of transmission of the AIDS virus is through sexual intercourse without a contraceptive barrier such as a condom. In fact, over 30 percent of the women who have the disease acquired it through sexual contact with a person who has AIDS or who is at risk for AIDS (Guinan and Hardy, 1987). What is noteworthy is that this pattern of heterosexually acquired AIDS parallels the distribution of traditional sexually transmitted diseases (Mays and Cochran, 1988; Moss and Kreiss, 1990; Cates and Toomey, 1990). A review of the literature indicates there was an epidemic of STDs in the African-American community long before there was HIV, and this problem continues to persist in spite of the belief that STDs may be a co-factor for HIV and AIDS. For example, although African-Americans made up 12 percent of the U.S. population in the 1980 census, recent data show that African-Americans accounted for 76 percent of the syphilis cases, 78 percent of the gonorrhea cases, and 28 percent of the AIDS cases (CDC, 1991a; Moran et al., 1988).

Due to the alarming increase in the incidence of AIDS and other STDs among African-Americans, there has been a constant need to develop immediate solutions. Unfortunately, little action has been taken, and it is apparent that we have not been successful in convincing African-Americans to use condoms to lower their risk of exposure to AIDS. As a result, we are now faced with a deadly disease that is wreaking havoc and spreading through sexual contact at a rate that has reached epidemic proportions. Our failure to address the issue of STDs in the past has come to haunt us in the present. Since condom usage is an effective means of reducing the spread of STDs including HIV/AIDS, there is a strong need to determine the attitudes about the use of condoms among African-American women who may be at high risk of becoming infected.

At the present time, there is a notable lack of data regarding the attitudes and beliefs about condom usage among African-American women. Most studies examining such variables have done so using male subjects or reported data for groups which include African-Americans without describing whether or not there were important ethnic differences in the relationships between condom usage and factors thought to be related to the spread of HIV. The conclusions drawn from the few available studies suggest that less than 20 percent of the young adult population use condoms as a means of reducing STDs such as AIDS (Keller, Bartlett, Schleifer, Johnson, Pinner, and Delaney, 1991). Therefore, the present inquiry has three objectives. The first is to determine the attitudes and knowledge about condom usage among a subgroup of young African-American adult females who report that they "always use condoms with their partner(s)." A second objective is to determine whether attitudes and knowledge about condoms differ among two groups of African-American females who do not use condoms with their partners but vary in their intentions (low versus high) to use condoms. Finally, the study will determine whether knowledge about AIDS, drug use, angry reactions related to condom use (or lack of use), STDs, and "risky" sexual behaviors (e.g., anal intercourse, sex with prostitutes) varies with the steady use of condoms.

The rationale for testing for the relationships described above is the pressing need to aid in the reduction and prevention of HIV, STDs, and teen pregnancies in the African-American community. This study is also important because the majority of the women in our sample are single, college-educated, actively dating, and in the process of selecting a mate for marriage and sex from the small selection of African-American males. As these women are searching for potential mates for marriage and sex, it is possible that they may become involved in serial monogamous relationships, or willing to share the few "good men" available. These behaviors present additional concerns given that in today's society they may serve as risk factors for exposure to HIV. Consequently, it is apparent that there is a need for conducting more systematic research on the interrelationships between risky sexual practices, condom use, and knowledge about AIDS.

As was the case for African-American males, a female subject was classified as a Steady User of condoms if they responded "true" to the following statement: "Over the past 12 months my partner(s) and I always use condoms when we have sexual intercourse." Women who indicated they did not use condoms were further divided into two groups based on their response to a statement regarding their intentions to use condoms ("I intend to try condoms"). African-American women who indicated that they "agree" or "strongly agree" with the statement were considered to have high intentions to use condoms while subjects who indicated "strongly disagree" or "disagree" were considered to have low intentions to use condoms. African-American females who reported that they were undecided ($n = 34$) were not included in the analyses. Of the 121 women, 21 (17 percent) were classified as Steady Users of condoms, 25 (21 percent) were classified as Low Intenders, and 75 (62 percent) were classified as High Intenders. The chi-square analyses comparing the demographic variables of age, education, and marital status across all three groups were not significant.

Table 6.2
Sexual Behaviors and Attitudes of Black Women Who Vary in Their Intentions to Use Condoms

	Steady Users		Low Intenders		High Intenders		
Variables	Mean	SD	Mean	SD	Mean	SD	F-Tests
AIDS knowledge	25.2	17.4	23.6	5.3	24.6	6.6	.19
Condom attitudes	37.4	18.4	24.1	6.5	33.9	7.1	3.17**
Contraceptive	15.6	4.1	14.9	3.6	15.2	2.3	.31
Inconvenient	5.7	3.0	9.2	3.2	6.7	2.5	10.88***
Excites	12.5	3.6	10.2	2.6	11.4	2.3	4.09**
Interrupts	11.4	4.7	18.3	5.1	14.9	3.9	14.88***
Acceptable	18.3	4.7	16.1	3.4	17.6	2.9	2.62#
Angry reactions	25.5	9.7	29.3	7.4	26.4	5.9	1.96
Smoking	1.2	.9	1.4	1.1	1.4	1.2	.14
Drinking	2.8	1.0	2.4	1.2	2.3	1.1	1.56
Marijuana	1.1	.7	1.5	1.6	1.1	.4	2.56#
Crack	.9	.2	1.3	1.4	.9	.1	2.20
Cocaine	.9	.3	1.4	1.5	1.0	.3	3.45*

Variables	Steady Users	Low Intenders	High Intenders	Chi-Square
Anal sex	10%	13%	18%	.81
Sex with prostitute	0%	4%	3%	.78
Gonorrhea	0%	4%	7%	1.61
Syphilis	0%	0%	1%	.63
Herpes	0%	0%	3%	1.26
Genital warts	5%	4%	7%	.31
HIV/AIDS	10%	0%	1%	5.05#
Consider self at high risk	5%	4%	8%	.52

#$p < .10$; *$p < .05$; **$p < .01$; ***$p < .001$.

The results indicated that the three groups of women did not differ with regard to their overall knowledge about AIDS (see Table 6.2). Generally speaking, the majority of women in all three groups correctly responded to the basic facts about AIDS (e.g., what AIDS is and how it is transmitted). Furthermore, the great majority of African-American females in the Steady Users (95 percent), Low Intenders (96 percent) and High Intenders (93 percent) groups knew that using condoms was an effective means of reducing the chances of exposure to HIV infection.

Significant group differences were noted for scales that assessed attitudes about condoms, but certain attitudes about the use of condoms (e.g., using as a contraceptive) were very similar for women in the Steady Users and High Intenders groups. However, these two groups were significantly ($p < .01$) different in their beliefs that condoms are uncomfortable and interrupt sex. Women with low intentions to use condoms had significantly ($p < .05$) more intense angry reactions regarding the negotiation of condom use and significantly more negative attitudes (e.g., discomfort for both partners, would object if partner wants to use) about the use of condoms than women in the other groups.

The three groups were not consistently differentiated by drug use, previous treatment for STDs, or their perceived risk for being exposed to AIDS. Steady Users were significantly less likely to feel condom use interrupted pleasure (Interruption, $F = 14.18$, $p < .001$) or was inconvenient (Inconvenience, $F = 10.80$, $p < .001$) compared to the High and Low Intenders groups. Steady Users were more likely to feel that condoms add to the excitement of sex (Excitement, $F = 4.09$, $p < .01$). The three groups did not differ in their attitudes about using condoms as a contraceptive (Contraceptive subscale).

Steady Users and High Intenders did not differ from each other in their acceptance of condoms. Further, Steady Users and High Intenders group members differed significantly in their views that condoms are uncomfortable and interrupt sex, while High Intender respondents were more likely to present negative attitudes with regard to this issue compared with Steady Users ($t = -3.02$, $p < .01$). The Steady Users and High Intenders groups differed significantly from the Low Intenders group in viewing condoms as uncomfortable and interruptive of sex ($t = -4.69$, $p < .001$; $t = 3.04$, $p < .01$). Finally, the Steady Users and High Intenders groups differed significantly from the Low Intenders group in perceiving condoms as less inconvenient ($t = -3.83, 3.54$; $p < .001$). In general, the overall pattern of the findings indicates that the Steady Users and High Intenders groups had significantly more positive attitudes about condoms than the Low Intenders group.

In other analyses, the total scale score and individual items of the Condoms Emotional Reaction Scale (CERS) for the three groups of women were compared using three-way analysis of variance (ANOVAS) and subsequent t-tests. The results revealed that the three groups were not significantly different from each other with regard to the total CERS scale score. However, the analyses of the individual items revealed that the groups differed on 6 of the 13 items [condoms may be uncomfortable for their partner ($F = 3.95$, $p < .05$); condoms may prevent their partners from reaching orgasm ($F = 4.19$, $p > .01$); condoms interrupt foreplay ($F = 7.66$, $p < .001$); partner refuses to engage in sexual intercourse unless a condom is used ($F = 6.31$, $p < .01$); when seen purchasing condoms ($F = 4.57$, $p < .01$); and when partner insists on not wearing a condom ($F = 4.56$, $p < .01$)].

Steady Users reported lower feelings of anger than the Low Intenders group when they perceived that their partner might not reach orgasm while wearing a condom ($t = -2.00$, $p < .05$) and when they thought that the use of a condom would interrupt foreplay ($t = -2.67$, $p < .01$). Steady Users also reported greater anger intensity than Low Intender respondents when their partner insisted on not wearing a condom ($t = 2.39$, $p < .05$). Subsequent comparisons of the anger intensity scores of women in the Steady Users and High Intenders groups did not reveal any significant differences.

African-American women with high intentions reported greater anger than their Low Intender counterparts when their partner insisted on not wearing a condom ($t = -3.28$, $p < .01$). In contrast, High Intender women experienced significantly less anger than women with low intentions when seen purchasing condoms by someone they know ($t = 2.45$, $p < .05$), and when their partner refuses to engage in sexual intercourse unless a condom is used ($t = 2.75$, $p < .01$). African-American women with high intentions report less anger than women with low intentions when they perceive that using a condom may be uncomfortable for their partner ($t = 2.39$, $p < .05$), will interrupt foreplay ($t = 3.39$, $p < .001$), or prevent their partner from reaching orgasm ($t = 2.89$, $p < .01$).

Although the analyses did not reveal significant differences between the groups in the report of gonorrhea, herpes, or genital warts, insignificant trends in the data are noteworthy. Steady Users reveal no history of gonorrhea, herpes, or genital warts. On the other hand, Low Intender members report low incidences of treatment for gonorrhea (1 percent), while High Intender women report several instances of treatment for gonorrhea (7 percent), herpes (3 percent), and genital warts (7 percent).

African-American women in the Low Intenders and High Intenders groups reported a greater percentage ($p < .05$) of involvement with multiple sex partners (i.e., sexual relations with at least four different partners over a 12-month period). The groups did not differ in the percentage of reported anal intercourse or sex with a prostitute. Interestingly, 10 percent of the Steady Users reported testing positive for AIDS, while only 1 percent of High Intender women and none of the Low Intender women reported a positive test. However, these differences were only marginally ($p < .10$) significant. Whereas patterns of drug use moderately distinguished the three groups, main effects for groups were noted for cocaine use ($F = 3.45$, $p < .05$), while marginal differences between the three groups were found for marijuana use ($F = 2.56$, $p < .10$). Low Intender group members reported greater use of both marijuana and cocaine than either the High Intenders or Steady Users groups.

The three groups also differed in their perceived vulnerability for contracting HIV. A significantly greater percentage of women in the Low Intenders and High Intenders groups believed that "condoms were not necessary if you love your partner," while no one in the Steady Users group felt that statement to be true ($p < .05$). The percentage of Steady Users (48 percent) who were "not worried about getting AIDS" was higher ($p < .05$) than those in the Low Intenders (26 percent) or the High Intenders (24 percent) groups. Finally, there was no significant group difference in the percentage of African-American women who perceived themselves to be in an AIDS high risk group.

SUMMARY AND DISCUSSION OF THE FINDINGS FOR FEMALES

The consensus among AIDS researchers is that African-American women are the fastest growing group at risk for contracting the AIDS virus (Mays and Cochran, 1988). A major reason for this is that women are engaging in unprotected sexual intercourse with a partner who is either at risk or infected with HIV and thus are exposing themselves to a high possibility of infection. It is important to realize that the risky sexual practices that contribute to the spread of HIV/AIDS is not a phenomenon that has recently come to our attention. It is a continuation of a problem that has been apparent in the African-American community for many years. For example, the spread of STDs has been increasing at an alarming rate within the African-American community for decades.

Recent information about the prevalence of gonorrhea and syphilis shows that African-Americans account for over 75 percent of both diseases while whites account for less than 16 percent of each (Moran et al., 1988). In the case of gonorrhea, for example, the rates per 100,000 population is 1,801 for African-Americans compared to 54 for whites. Current evidence suggests that STDs may be co-factors for HIV/AIDS (Moss and Kreiss, 1990). It is only now with the latest STD (AIDS) that can we ascertain the devastating effect of an ignored problem. The question we must ask is why, if the rate of infection of STDs has been at an enormously high level for many years, do people continue to engage in sexual intercourse without the use of a contraceptive barrier such as a condom? Equally important is the answer to other questions about whether knowledge of the transmission of HIV/AIDS or fears and anxieties about being exposed to HIV/AIDS is related to condom usage.

Three important findings were discovered in this inquiry. First, the data show that there is no significant relationship between knowledge about AIDS and condom usage for African-American women. Knowledge about AIDS is no different among women who do not use or who intend to use condoms as compared to African-American women who report that they always use condoms. It appears that African-American college students are extremely knowledgeable about AIDS yet they fail to take precautionary measures such as using condoms or reducing the number of sex partners to prevent infection with HIV. That they are not utilizing their knowledge to make decisions about safe sexual practices, and that they willingly continue to engage in behaviors that are putting themselves and their partner(s) at risk is without question.

Previous studies have found that knowledge about AIDS-related risks does not necessarily translate into AIDS risk-reduction behaviors (Mays and Cochran, 1988). Although education and prevention are important, some of us in health psychology and public health realize that we have not created a "culturally sensitive" atmosphere that motivates African-American women to use condoms or to make changes in other behaviors which lowers their risk of being exposed to STDs. The typical explanation given for the lack of association between knowledge and risky behavior is that young adults view themselves as invincible (Perlof, 1983; Elkind, 1978). While this is likely to be part of the reason, we do not really know why the gap between knowledge and risky behavior is so large among African-Americans or other ethnic groups. Perhaps one possible reason was discovered in a study by Ripley (1985) which revealed that AIDS knowledge-based information presented to young adults in a written manner is far less effective than information presented audiovisually (e.g., videotapes) or in conjunction with audiovisual material.

To date, most of the information that has been disseminated throughout the African-American community has been in the form of pamphlets and other written material. In an age where television programming such as "MTV" and "The Simpsons" have a far greater impact on our young adult population than the daily newspaper, we may need to redirect our educational efforts by incorporating methods (e.g., videos, television) to which young adults can relate. Only then can such media impact this generation by changing attitudes and causing individuals to challenge their own personal beliefs that they maintain about the level of risk associated with their behaviors. It is my belief that important personal attitudes and convictions must be changed before the level of HIV/AIDS related knowledge can be significantly linked to concurrent reductions in risky sexual behaviors.

The second major finding uncovered in this inquiry shows that a larger percentage of Steady Users (10 percent) have tested positive for AIDS compared to the Low (0 percent) and High (1 percent) Intenders groups. This is in contrast to what was predicted since it was expected that exposure to HIV/AIDS would be greater among women who report that they do not consistently use condoms. However, from these data it may be concluded that African-American women with HIV/AIDS appear to be using condoms to prevent their partners from being exposed to the virus. Perhaps the problem which we encounter in this study is that we really do not know if people are telling the truth. It is impossible to know if the women who are HIV positive have informed their partners of their health status and the potential risk associated with having sexual relationships with a person who has HIV/AIDS. Factors associated with the extent and seriousness of the relationships (i.e., being married and engaged) as well as the degree of happiness and honesty are possibly related to how open the women with HIV/AIDS have been with their partners.

Although the women with HIV/AIDS may be using a condom during sexual intercourse, it was not possible to determine whether they are using condoms during other kinds of sexual contact (i.e., anal sex, oral sex). Despite these limiting factors, we have little reason to doubt the accuracy and reliability of the data, except to say that we have to put much faith in the belief that people, under the right circumstances that protect their privacy and confidentiality, will openly disclose factual information about their sexuality.

While it is important that African-American women engage in health practices that will decrease the chance of their partner becoming infected with HIV, it is apparent that the existing public health prevention messages are not working effectively to prevent exposure to HIV/AIDS. It is without question that a major priority for women (and men) with HIV/AIDS is to focus on preventing the virus from spreading to others. However, there is a strong need to focus on primary prevention as well, so that women will never be exposed to this deadly virus in the first place. As indicated earlier, the use of other media sources (e.g., visual, videotapes) to disseminate HIV/AIDS-related information may be more useful in changing attitudes and behaviors related to the prevention of risky sexual behaviors among members of the African-American community.

The third major finding revealed that the responses to the individual items on the anger questionnaire support the beliefs that: (1) condoms are uncomfortable, and (2) that part of this discomfort is reflected by intense angry reactions associated with the use of condoms. The data revealed some unique findings which may give some indication as to why women, particularly those with low intentions, do not use condoms. For example, the data show that these women not only do not use condoms, but they report being angered when they are seen purchasing condoms. Perhaps they feel embarrassed or think that others may consider them a bit loose and sexually uninhibited or liberated for buying condoms. Given the high prevalence of teenage pregnancies and children born to African-American women who are single, it may be that there is a relatively large group of African-American women who become angry and upset about obtaining any contraceptive protection.

Interestingly enough, women with low intentions to use condoms do not get angry and upset when their partners insist on not using a condom. It may be that these women feel a false sense of security when their partner(s) says that he does not want to use a condom. Perhaps their partner's insistence on not using a condom contributes to these women feeling and believing that their partner is safe, otherwise he would not be so persistent in "not using" a condom. These women may also feel that their partner(s) trust them and think they are safe. In general, the angry reaction (or lack thereof) may create a false sense of security that may have fatal consequences.

Since it appears that knowledge about AIDS (or lack thereof) is not significantly related to risky sexual behaviors, we must therefore look for the next possible solution. Perhaps we must look not at what the women know about condoms and AIDS but how the use of condoms fits into their lives. In this study it was revealed that women are knowledgeable about condoms, especially as a form of contraception. What we did not look at is the use of condoms as a method of protection from AIDS in their everyday lives. From this study as well as the statistics about the spread of STDs and teenage pregnancies in the African-American community, it is readily apparent that the use of condoms plays a very small part in the habitual lives of these women. These data suggest that the next step would be to find a way to incorporate the use of condoms into the everyday lives of the women. Perhaps new marketing concepts or slogans that glorify the erotic nature of condom usage are needed to encourage women to use condoms. This was exemplified in a study by Tanner and Pollack (1988) in which subjects who were given erotic instructions concerning the use of condoms had more positive attitudes and showed an increase in the pleasure they derived from using condoms. On the other hand, the subjects that were given no instructions had more negative reactions about using condoms.

It is important for the media to use the information derived from this and other studies to create a more effective intervention strategy. To aid in the battle against AIDS it may be necessary for the media to take an active role in disseminating information to the African-

American community. To date, this has been an area of neglect for both white and African-American media. The white media attempts to be "colorblind" and ignore the culturally-specific realities of the African-American population, while the African-American media has done an even graver disservice through their refusal to recognize the association between African-Americans and sexually transmitted diseases that are associated with sexual behaviors (e.g., anal intercourse, oral sex) that may be considered deviant. For example, the leading magazines in the African-American community, *Ebony* and *Essence,* carried no articles on AIDS until the spring of 1987. Moreover, the *Journal of the National Medical Association* (the professional organization of black physicians) carried their first article on AIDS in 1986 which was only a short guest editorial (Hammonds, 1987).

ANGRY REACTIONS, CONDOM USE, AND SEXUAL BEHAVIORS

There is no doubt among sex researchers and the public that the experience of high levels of negative emotions such as anger and irritability is one of the major reasons for sexual performance problems such as premature ejaculation and impotence in males and vaginitis and lack of orgasm in women. As my research and the research of others have revealed (Johnson, 1990a; Tavris, 1982; Williams, 1989), the physiological responses associated with the experience of anger, irritability, and anxiety have a deleterious impact on the body and severely impair cognitive processes and our ability to make rational decisions and solve problems. Even though the role of anger, irritability, and other emotions, as causative factors in problems such as child and spouse abuse have been widely recognized, very little attention has been given as to whether such emotions are related to risky sexual behaviors or to the extent to which these emotional states interfere with the negotiation of safe sex practices such as using condoms to lower the risk of being exposed to the HIV/AIDS virus. Therefore, the purpose of this section is to determine whether condom usage, sexual behaviors, perception of AIDS risk, and drug usage are significantly different among individuals who vary in the intensity of their anger.

For the purpose of this inquiry, three angry reaction groups were formed based on the responses of the subjects to ten questions that assessed the intensity of anger in relationship to condom use. The groups were formed by breaking the total distribution of the sample into approximately equal thirds. As a consequence, subjects with scores less than 15 on the Condom Emotional Reaction Scale (35 percent) constituted the Low Group, subjects with scores between 16 and 21 (32 percent) constituted the Moderate Group, and those

Table 6.3
Condom Usage Attitudes, AIDS Knowledge, and Drug Use as a Function of Angry Reactions

| Variables | Women | | | | | | Men | | | | | | F-Tests | |
| | Low (61%) | | Medium (59%) | | High (39%) | | Low (39%) | | Medium (40%) | | High (61%) | | Group | Group x Gender |
	Mean	SD	Mean	SD	Mean	SD	Mean	SD	Mean	SD	Mean	SD		
Condom attitudes														
Contraceptive	13.7	4.9	15.6	2.2	16.2	2.9	14.4	5.1	16.3	2.9	15.9	3.2	9.25***	.55
Interrupts	13.3	5.8	13.5	4.5	17.1	5.5	13.2	5.2	16.0	4.1	20.1	4.9	32.78***	2.78#
Acceptance	16.4	5.4	18.3	3.1	17.9	2.9	16.7	5.2	18.6	2.6	15.8	3.1	7.17***	2.83#
Excites	10.5	3.8	11.9	2.7	11.5	2.9	10.8	4.0	12.2	3.2	11.8	2.6	5.20**	.00
Inconvenient	6.0	3.1	6.5	2.5	8.5	3.1	6.0	2.6	8.0	2.6	10.6	3.4	42.80***	3.34*
Total scale														
Perceived risk	3.0	1.1	3.3	.9	3.2	.9	3.2	1.1	3.2	1.1	3.0	1.1	.64	.68
AIDS knowledge	24.9	2.7	24.1	2.3	21.2	3.2	23.4	4.6	23.0	5.7	21.2	6.8	4.83**	1.07
Smoking	1.1	.8	1.5	1.1	1.7	1.5	1.2	.7	1.6	1.3	1.5	1.4	3.84*	.49
Drinking	2.3	1.2	2.6	1.1	2.4	1.1	2.6	1.6	3.0	1.2	2.7	1.5	1.66	.04
Marijuana	.9	.5	1.4	1.1	1.2	.6	1.2	.7	1.5	.9	1.9	1.9	8.28***	2.50#
Crack	.9	.3	1.1	.9	1.0	0.0	.9	.3	1.1	.3	1.4	1.6	4.10**	1.95
Cocaine	.9	.4	1.2	.9	1.0	0.0	.9	.3	1.1	.6	1.4	1.6	3.81*	1.91
Angry reactions	10.8	5.1	18.4	1.6	25.2	3.4	10.1	4.6	18.4	1.5	25.6	3.7	398.42***	.58
Always use condoms	25%		29%		24%		40%		33%		35%			
Condoms not necessary if you love your partner	11%		16%		26%		11%		16%		35%			

#$p < .10$; *$p < .05$; **$p < .01$; ***$p < .001$.

subjects with scores greater than 22 (32 percent) constituted the High Group. Given the fact that males scored significantly higher than females on the Condom Emotional Reaction Scale, it was predicted that there would be significant differences in the percentage of males and females in the Low and High Groups. It was also predicted that the Low, Moderate, and High Groups would differ significantly from each other in their attitudes about the use of condoms and other sexual behaviors.

Table 6.3 shows the average condom attitude scores of the five condom attitudes subscales and the total scale scores for males and females with Low, Moderate (Medium), and High angry reactions. A chi-square analysis was conducted to compare the percentage of males and females in the three angry reactions groups. The results revealed ($x^2 = 12.00$, $p < .001$) that there was a greater percentage of males in the High Group (61 percent) and females in the Low Group (61 percent). Further analyses showed that the three groups were significantly different on the total scale score ($p < .001$) of the condom attitude questionnaire and each of the subscales ($p < .001$). For the most part, the pattern of the relationships between condom attitudes and the degree of angry reactions about the use of condoms was somewhat linear. In other words, the attitudes were more negative for both males and females in the Moderate and High Angry Reactions Groups. Neither of the interactions between Angry Reactions Groups and Gender were significant.

The comparison of the AIDS knowledge scores for the groups was conducted using analysis of variance procedures. The results revealed that subjects in the High Angry Reaction Group had significantly lower knowledge scores than subjects in the Low and Moderate Groups. This pattern was consistent for both males and females. Even though knowledge about the cause and transmission of AIDS was significantly lower among subjects in the High Angry Reactions Group, there were no significant differences between the groups in their perceived risk of being exposed to the HIV/AIDS virus. Finally, certain drug use (cigarettes, marijuana, crack, and cocaine) was uniformly higher among subjects in the High Angry Reactions Group. Whereas this pattern was true for both males and females, the findings were more consistent for males who use marijuana and crack.

The information concerning the sexual behavior of the male and female subjects in the three Angry Reactions Groups are presented in Table 6.4. Chi-square analyses were used to compare the percentage of subjects in the three groups who engaged in the particular sexual behaviors. As can be observed, both males and females in the High Angry Reactions Groups were more likely to engage in anal

Table 6.4
Risky Sexual Behaviors and Sexually Transmitted Diseases as a Function of Angry Reactions

	Men			Women			
Variables	Low	Med	High	Low	Med	High	Chi-Square
Anal intercourse	5	18	31	7	11	20	18.40**
Oral sex	42	54	64	25	45	42	18.95**
Sex with prostitutes	8	16	29	0	0	8	38.59***
Four or more partners	51	6	52	15	2	22	39.99***
HIV/AIDS	5	3	11	3	2	0	8.94
Gonorrhea	16	8	26	3	2	14	23.63***
Syphilis	3	3	14	0	4	3	15.75***
Herpes	3	3	11	0	2	6	14.12***
Genital warts	3	5	11	2	5	8	5.60

$**p < .01$; $***p < .001$.

and oral sex compared to their counterparts who had low and moderate angry reactions about the use of condoms. A large percentage of males (35 percent) and females (26 percent) in the High Angry Reactions Group believe that "condoms are not necessary if you love your partner." These percentages were significantly larger ($x^2 = 13.99$, $p < .01$) than the percentage of males and females in the Low and Moderate Groups who held similar views. Be that as it may, there was no significant difference in the percentage of males or females in the three Angry Reactions Groups who reported that they "always" use condoms. Roughly one-third of the males and females in each of the three groups reported that they "always" use condoms.

A significantly larger percentage of males in the High Angry Reactions Group reported having sex with prostitutes (29 percent). A similar pattern was noted for females, with 8 percent of the women in the High Angry Reactions Group reporting that they have sex with prostitutes. Among the males, having sex with prostitutes was also very prevalent among members of the Low (8 percent) and Moderate (16 percent) Angry Reactions Groups. Males in each of the three groups were also more likely to be involved sexually with four or more partners. However, it was the males in the Moderate Group who were most likely to be involved with four or more sexual partners. The opposite was true for females with the percentage of females who are involved with four or more partners being significantly lower for subjects in the Moderate Group and highest for African-American females in the High Angry Reactions Group.

Information about the relationship between angry reactions and sexually transmitted diseases are also presented in Table 6.4. Chi-square analyses were used to compare the percentage of subjects in the three groups who had been exposed to the various STDs. Among the males, the data indicate that subjects in the High Angry Reactions Group were significantly ($p < .001$) more likely to have been exposed to gonorrhea (26 percent), syphilis (14 percent), and herpes (11 percent), compared to males in the Low (3 to 16 percent) and Moderate (3 to 8 percent) Groups. There was also a strong tendency for males in the High Angry Reactions Group to be more likely to be exposed to genital warts (11 percent) and the HIV/AIDS virus (11 percent), compared to males in the Low (3 to 5 percent) and Moderate (3 to 5 percent) Groups.

Among the females, significant associations between angry reactions about condoms and STDs were also noted. For example, a larger percentage of females in the High Angry Reactions Group had been exposed to gonorrhea (14 percent), compared to women in the Low (3 percent) and Moderate (2 percent) Groups. A similar pattern was observed for syphilis, herpes, and genital warts. However, the relationship between angry reactions and HIV/AIDS were the opposite of what was expected, with essentially no women in the High Angry Reactions Group being exposed to the HIV/AIDS virus compared to 3 percent for the Low Group and 2 percent for the Moderate Angry Reactions Group.

In general, the overall pattern of the findings presented in Table 6.4 shows that both males and females who respond with intense angry reactions about the use of condoms (High Angry Reactions Group) are more likely to engage in risky sexual behaviors (e.g., anal intercourse, sex with prostitutes, having four or more partners) that increase the possibility of being exposed to the HIV/AIDS virus. In these particular cases it is unknown whether the angry reactions are a response to the partners refusal to use a condom or whether the individuals dislike and experience discomfort with the use of condoms. While these data are correlational in nature, and it is difficult to determine the direction of causality, it appears that the negative attitudes of the individual lead to the intense angry reactions about the use of condoms. Evidence for this conclusion is based on the fact that both male and female subjects in the High Angry Reactions Group had a strong dislike of using condoms. They expressed very strong attitudes about condoms being uncomfortable, inconvenient, and interruptive of sex. Nevertheless, one of the end results for both males and females with intense angry reactions about the use of condoms is a higher probability of being exposed to sexually transmitted diseases, including the HIV/AIDS virus.

As indicated earlier, the interpersonal and health problems related to the poor management of anger have been well documented for

African-Americans and other ethnic groups. However, there are no published investigations of the interrelationships between anger, condom use, and sexual behaviors. The findings of the present inquiry clearly show that risky sexual behaviors and STDs are significantly related to intense angry reactions associated with the potential use of condoms. However, condom use did not vary as a function of the intensity of angry reactions. As a consequence, angry reactions associated with the use of condoms appear to be more strongly related to risky sexual behaviors and STDs rather than the use (or lack thereof) of condoms. Therefore, the data suggest that negative attitudes and the discomfort associated with the use of condoms should be targets for intervention. It may be possible that negative attitudes about the use of condoms may act synergistically or interact with angry reactions to contribute to condoms not being used during sexual intercourse. While this possibility exists, the extent to which it is true needs further verification. There is also a strong need for future research to investigate the possibility that the modification of angry reactions using behavioral therapy techniques may lower the engagement in other risky sexual behaviors.

Among African-Americans, conflicts about the management and expression of anger have been significantly related to stressful life events such as divorce or marital difficulties, job and economic problems, problems with family members, with the law, and loss of friends (Broman and Johnson, 1988). Individuals who have problems managing their anger also behave in ways that enhance hostile interactions with others and generate greater psychological distress (e.g., increased levels of depression and anxiety, inability to concentrate) for themselves. The findings that anger conflict is related to a greater number of life events is supported by the argument that people who experience difficulty in handling their anger are more likely to destroy important supportive relationships and networks with others, relationships that serve to "buffer" or mediate between negative life events and unhealthy health practices.

It can be argued that risky sexual behaviors (i.e., anal intercourse, having sex with prostitutes, having four or more sex partners) could be related to increased anger that results from the strained and unbalanced pattern of interactions with a partner or significant other. In other words, the intense angry reactions may be a marker or cue for deeper interpersonal problems which result in behaviors that may serve to create distance between the two people involved in the relationship. For example, several of the items making up the CERS appear to tap into areas that may be perceived as being very touchy or threatening for couples to deal with (e.g., partner refuses sex unless a condom is used, partner makes inquiries about previous sexual behavior). In these cases, the intense angry reactions may be a result of the person feeling insulted and not trusted by their partner who is making inquiries about previous sexual behaviors and who has refused to have sex unless a condom is used. Be this as it may, the end result is the creation of a "psychological distance" between the couple which could lead one or both partners to seek out other avenues for sexual expression (e.g., having more than one partner, having sex with a prostitute).

CHAPTER 7

Drug Use and Perceived Risk of Being Exposed to AIDS

It has been argued that approximately 95 percent of the present American AIDS patients fall within one of the five identified risk groups. The largest risk group, which accounts for about 65 percent of all adult AIDS cases, consists of homosexual or bisexual men. Gay men who are also IV-drug users account for approximately 8 percent of additional AIDS cases, while heterosexual IV-drug users represent approximately 17 percent of AIDS cases. Hemophiliacs (1 percent), other persons with a history of blood transfusions (2 percent), and individuals who contracted AIDS during heterosexual activities (4 percent), represent other high-risk groups (CDC, 1990a, 1990b, 1990c, 1991a, 1991b). The approximately 3 percent of American AIDS cases that do not fall within one of these groups may include persons who are not candid concerning their risk experiences and persons who are not aware of their sexual exposure to AIDS. According to these figures, the use of the so called "hard drugs" is associated with the transmission of AIDS in approximately 25 percent of the AIDS cases. For these individuals, the transmission of AIDS occurs as a function of the exposure risk behaviors of people rather than because of the membership in a high-risk group. In other words, IV-drug users are at high risk for AIDS exposure only when they share or reuse needles and are exposed to HIV-infected blood from previous users of the same needle. However, the use of non-IV drugs such as alcohol, marijuana, and cocaine are likely to play a role in the transmission of the AIDS virus because their use during sex is likely to increase the odds that an individual will engage in risky sexual practices because these drugs lead to sexual uninhibitedness and poor judgment.

The cumulative incidence of AIDS cases from 1981 to 1988 was 13.6 times higher among African-American women than in any other group of women (Quinn, 1990). African-American women are at greater risk for acquiring an HIV infection because of AIDS-related risk behaviors (e.g., IV-drug use), less knowledge of AIDS, and fewer available health resources (Flaskerud and Nyamathi, 1989; Mays and Cochran, 1988). Among all cases of AIDS in women, 85 percent occurred among women of childbearing age (CDC, 1990a, 1991a; Chu, et al., 1990), with prenatal transmission (i.e., the case where the child is exposed to the virus via its mother's bloodstream) ranging from 30 percent to 50 percent among children born of seropositive mothers (Quinn, 1990; Saunders, 1989). In general, almost all of the other pediatric AIDS cases occurred because the child was exposed during delivery, or because the child received transfusions of infected blood. It has been estimated that a cumulative total of as many as 10 million infants will be born infected with HIV worldwide by the year 2000 ("AIDS Among Women," 1991).

African-American female prostitutes have higher HIV seroprevalence than prostitutes of other ethnic groups ("Antibody to human immunodeficiency virus in female prostitutes," 1987), while African-American female IV-drug users have higher rates of HIV seropositivity than whites, and, in some instances, than African-American males (Lange, Snyder, Lozovsky, et al., 1988; Lewis and Watters, 1988). Moreover, African-American female IV-drug users, once stricken with HIV, appear to have the shortest life expectancy of all the major ethnic and risk groups (Rothenberg, Woelfel, Stoneburner, et al., 1987).

A study of 155 IV-drug users by Lewis and Watters (1989) was completed to attempt to explain why African-American female IV-drug users are more likely to test HIV antibody positive. The results revealed that African-American women had higher HIV seroprevalence than white women (21 percent compared to 7 percent, respectively, odds ratio 3.59, 95 percent CI 1.28–9.98). To attempt to explain the ethnic difference, the distribution of a series of risk factors associated with HIV seropositivity, such as needle sharing, high-risk sexual behavior, and history of STDs were examined. The results revealed that there was either no significant difference between African-Americans and whites or white IV-drug users were more likely than African-Americans to engage in specific risky behaviors such as needle sharing or to have an STD history. Fewer African-American women than white women reported regular sexual contact with bisexual partners, but they (African-American women) were more likely to express uncertainty about the sexual orientation of their partner— that is knowing for certain if their partner was bisexual. The results of this study also revealed that a higher proportion of African-American IV-drug users reported unprotected sexual contacts than whites, although the difference was not significant.

Across the nation, the major source of HIV infection among African-American women is IV-drug abuse followed closely by heterosexual contact, particularly with partners who are IV-drug abusers (Mays and Cochran, 1988; Saunders, 1989). For example, among African-American women with AIDS, 56 percent had a history of IV-drug abuse, while 33 percent had sex partners who were at increased risk for, or known to be infected with, HIV. There is no doubt that IV-drug abuse is high among minority populations where drug dealing is a very prevalent means for providing easy money for women and children who have few means of earning a living (Mays and Cochran, 1988; Worth and Rodriguez, 1987). The fact that the CDC (1991a, 1991b, 1991c) reports that approximately 40 percent of IV-drug abusers with AIDS are African-Americans lends support to the belief that drugs are readily accessible in the African-American community. While it is true that the behavior of IV-drug users (e.g., sharing dirty needles) increases the chance of being exposed to the AIDS virus, it is also true that the prevalence of AIDS among African-American IV-drug users is in part related to other risky behaviors such as exchanging sex for drugs or having multiple sex partners (Flaskerud and Nyamathi, 1989).

Ostrow (1990) highlighted several hypotheses linking substance abuse and risk-taking behaviors including the following: (a) drug use inhibits normal self-protective barriers to risk taking; (b) drug use and risk taking are related to common personality characteristics (e.g., sensation seeking, rebelliousness); (c) drug use enhances the physical sensations of sex, thereby reinforcing the likelihood of their co-occurrence and the likelihood of all types of sexual behaviors occurring; and (d) concurrent drug use and risky sexual behaviors are strongly determined by social context factors.

Stall, McKusick, Wiley, Coates, and Ostrow (1986) found that risky sexual activity was positively correlated with the use of particular drugs during sex (including alcohol, amyl nitrate, and marijuana), the number of drugs used during sexual activity, and the frequency of combining drugs and sex. Importantly, approximately 90 percent of the men in this study were well aware of what constituted risky sexual behaviors. In another study of a large group of 604 gay men in New York City (Martin, 1990), it was noted that both insertive and receptive anal intercourse was positively correlated with drug use over the period of the study. Marijuana was the most commonly used drug during sex, however, cocaine and amphetamine use were most strongly correlated with unprotected receptive and insertive anal intercourse. The most important finding was that the cessation of drug use during sex was associated with lower rates of risky sexual behaviors. In the 1986–87 time interval, Martin found that only cocaine use was significantly correlated with the frequency of risky sexual behaviors.

Among a sample of 340 African-American, sexually active adolescents (ages 15–19), the total number of drugs used predicted the number of sexually transmitted diseases ($r^2 = .20$) among the female crack users (Fullilove, Fullilove, et al., 1990a, 1990b). This research team also found that the exchange of sexual favors for drugs, and engaging in drug use during sex, were significant predictors of pregnacies for African-American crack users ($r^2 = .18$). Boyer and Schafer (1990) found that marijuana and alcohol use significantly predicted a lower frequency of condom use among a sample of 544 high school students. In this sample, 54 percent of the students reported that they use alcohol daily, while 6 percent reported a history of an STD diagnosis. Condoms were used by roughly 32 percent of the sample, but the majority of those who reported using condoms did not consistently use them.

In a study of 7,600 women drug users, Weissman (1990) found that 55 percent of non-IV-drug abusers were African-Americans, 24 percent used crack daily, and only 8 percent used condoms. Interestingly enough, crack use was correlated with an increased number of sexual partners, the use of sex as a source of income, and number of STD diagnoses. In another study of 157 pregnant ethnic minority women in Boston, researchers noted a 74 percent prevalence of crack use, 69 percent of their sample had multiple sexual partners, and 98 percent engaged in some high-risk sexual activity in the six-month period prior to pregnancy and during pregnancy (Hingson, Strunin, Craven, et al., 1989; Amaro, 1990). A striking 87 percent of these women reported a frequency of risky sexual behaviors of at least once per week over this period and 19 percent did so on a daily basis. These women revealed a history of STDs in 57 percent of cases, yet nearly 80 percent reported that there was little or no chance of themselves being exposed to AIDS.

Apart from HIV transmission among IV-drug users who share needles and exchange sex for drugs, research has focused on the role of chemical substance use or recreational drugs as a risk factor for AIDS. Among the substances that have been identified as differentially associated with AIDS (i.e., AIDS risk co-factors) are cigarette smoking, marijuana smoking, and the use of inhaled nitrites (Kelly and St. Lawrence, 1988; Marmor et al., 1982; Newell, Mansell, Wilson, Lynch, Spitz, and Hersh, 1985; Weber, Wadsworth, Rogers, Moshitael, Scott, McManus, Berrie, Jefferies, Harris, and Pinching, 1986). Of these substances, the greatest attention has been given to inhaled nitrites (Goedert, 1985; Newell et al., 1985). These drugs are usually referred to as poppers (amyl, butyl, and isobutyl nitrites) and are considered to be vasodilators that produce transient hypotension, flushing, light-headedness, and anesthesia when inhaled.

While amyl nitrites have long been used to provide relief from the pain caused by angina pectoris, they are now available without a prescription and are used by some people to enhance sexual pleasure. There is some evidence, based on animal studies, that inhaled nitrites are carcinogenic, and there is some evidence suggesting that nitrite use is associated with T-lymphocyte abnormalities in humans (Dax, Adler, Dorsey, and Jaffe, 1987; Goedert, Sarngadharan, Eyster, Weiss, Bodner, Gallo, and Blattner, 1985; Newell et al., 1985).

Even though the physiological risk-potentiating effects from nitrate inhalation cannot be ruled out, their role in the transmission of AIDS appears to be behavioral rather than chemical. The same is true for the use of other recreational drugs such as marijuana and the heavy use of alcohol (Stall, McKusick, Wiley, Coates, and Ostrow, 1986). In other words, the use of these substances at the time of sexual activity is related to increased probability of engaging in high-risk sexual practices. For example, inhaled nitrite use is common among individuals who engage in such high-risk sexual activities as receptive anal intercourse, perhaps because of the behavior-uninhibiting and mildly anesthetic effects (Siegel, Mesagno, Chen, and Christ, 1987; Stall et al., 1986; Stevens et al., 1987).

There is also a large amount of current research that has tied the use of drugs in black adolescents and young adults to STDs. For example, a study of black teenage crack users, 64 percent of whom reported attending school, revealed that 41 percent reported a history of STDs, with girls (55 percent) having a higher prevalence of STDs than boys (34 percent). The history of an STD was more likely to be reported by those combining the use of crack with sex. Moreover, boys were more likely than girls to give or receive sexual favors for drugs or money. In addition, 40 percent of those who exchanged sex for drugs engaged in sexual practices while high on crack. A number of these teenagers reported using other substances such as marijuana (92 percent) and alcohol (82 percent) daily (Fullilove, Fullilove, Bowser, and Gross, 1990a; Fullilove and Fullilove, 1989). Furthermore, 52 percent of those who combined crack with sex reported an STD, with gonorrhea, trichomonas, chlamydia, and genital warts being the most commonly reported (Fullilove et al., 1990a).

Results of a study of inner city black adolescents indicate that drug use was reported more often among the sexually active students in both the clinic and school sample. The most common drug reported was marijuana, with 52 percent of the clinic sample and 75 percent of the school sample reporting exclusive use of this drug. Cocaine was the second most common drug, with 31 percent and 19 percent of the clinic and school samples respectively reporting use (Keller et al., 1991).

Although previous research suggests that drug use is significantly related to the STD epidemic in black adolescents, comparison studies of adolescents of varying ethnicities have revealed that substance use among blacks is substantially lower than whites and Native Americans (Bachman, Wallace, O'Malley, Johnston, Kurth, and Neighbors, 1991; Johnson and Gilbert, 1991). More specifically, the study of smoking, drinking, and illicit drug use among high school seniors (Bachman et al., 1991) revealed that the prevalence rates for marijuana were highest among Native American and white students, while lower among blacks and Puerto Ricans. Similarly, the prevalence rates for cocaine were much lower for black students than all other groups with the exception of Asian males and females. Even so, the rates for black females remained lower than this group. Again, with alcohol and other illicit drugs, rates among whites and Native Americans were relatively high compared to blacks.

A study of inner-city African-American and white students in junior and senior high school also indicated that levels of cigarette, alcohol, and hard drug use were significantly higher among white students irrespective of gender. Over 71 percent and 56 percent of African-American males and females over 16 years old respectively reported never smoking. Similarly, approximately 58 percent and 60 percent of African-American males and females reported never drinking, 73 percent and 61 percent never smoking marijuana, and 96 percent and 98 percent never doing hard drugs. There was a general trend for drug use to be correlated with higher sexual activity in both groups (Zabin et al., 1986).

For most drugs and most ethnic groups fewer females than males reported use. For black students, this gender difference was found for all major drugs (alcohol, marijuana, cocaine, and cigarettes). These data have led investigators to suggest that the spread of STDs among blacks may be independent of drug use, given that white adolescents are unaffected by STDs to the same extent as blacks (Zabin, Hardy, Smith, and Hirsch, 1986; Bachman, Wallace, O'Malley, Johnston, Kurth, and Neighbors, 1991). These data are not to suggest that drug use does not influence STDs given that their uninhibiting effects impair judgment and consequently may increase risk for STD transmission (Kelly and St. Lawrence, 1988), but simply to emphasize that other variables besides drug use may be associated with the transmission of STDs, including HIV among African-Americans. The interrelationships of such variables (i.e., lack of condom use, having multiple sex partners) have not been studied in young heterosexual adults who vary in the risk factors described above. It seems that an increase in risk factors may result in a concurrent increase in risk for HIV exposure.

RELATIONSHIPS BETWEEN DRUG USE, SEXUAL BEHAVIORS, AND ATTITUDES FOR AFRICAN-AMERICAN MALES

The percentage of African-American males who use drugs is presented in Table 2.1, while the data presented in Table 7.1 shows the Pearson product-moment correlations between the various measures of drug use and sexual behaviors for African-American males and females. In these analyses, drug use is kept as a continuous variable so as to determine the relationships between the frequency of use and sexual behaviors. The measures of PCP (angel dust) and heroin simply reflect whether the respondents have ever used the substance and not the frequency of use. In general, the percentage of subjects who reported using PCP and heroin were quite low.

The data for males clearly shows that smoking cigarettes and drinking are consistently not significantly related to AIDS knowledge or attitudes about the use of condoms. Drinking was significantly related to having multiple sex partners, having sex with prostitutes, and having beliefs about being at increased risk of being exposed to HIV/AIDS, although the correlations are small in magnitude. Small significant correlations were also found for the associations between certain sexually transmitted diseases and both smoking cigarettes and drinking. Interestingly enough, smoking cigarettes was found to be significantly correlated with having HIV/AIDS.

The use of marijuana was found to be more consistently associated with having STDs, particulary genital warts where the correlation was $r = .26$ and significant at the $p < .001$ level. The use of crack and cocaine were found to be primarily correlated with being angry about the use of condoms during sexual intercourse, having a history of STDs, and having HIV/AIDS. Of all the drugs, PCP and heroin use were found to be highly significantly correlated with risky sexual behaviors, STDs, HIV/AIDS, as well as having beliefs about being at high-risk for being exposed to HIV/AIDS. Both PCP and heroin were more strongly associated with the practice of anal intercourse. However, the associations with STDs were remarkably strong with most correlations being significant at the $p < .0001$ level. These were the only drugs that were significantly correlated with AIDS knowledge. The overall pattern of the correlations indicates that individuals who reported using these drugs had a significantly lower level of under-

Table 7.1
Correlations between Drug Use, Sexual Behaviors, and Attitudes for African-American Males

Variables	Smoking	Drinking	Marijuana	Crack	Cocaine	PCP	Heroin
AIDS knowledge	.13	.03	.04	-.06	-.06	-.28***	-.33***
Condom attitudes	.08	.07	.01	.06	.06	.06	.07
Contraceptive	.09	.17*	.16#	.11	.11	-.03	-.01
Interrupt	.17*	.11	.17*	.10	.12	-.15#	-.13
Acceptance	.11	-.05	.02	-.02	-.01	.03	.03
Excitement	.04	.15#	.06	.06	.04	-.00	.05
Inconvenient	.17*	.16#	.18*	.10	.12	.15#	.12
Angry reactions	.20*	.04	.22**	.21**	.23**	.25**	.32***
Always use condoms	.01	.13	.20*	.01	.03	.05	.22**
Multiple partners	.09	.22**	.01	.16#	.12	.03	.05
Four partners in past year	.09	.24**	.07	.17*	.14	.03	-.04
Perceived risk	.09	.17*	.07	.08	.04	-.06	.06
High risk groups	.19*	.16#	.15#	-.08	-.12	.27***	.19*
Anal intercourse	.08	.02	.09	.04	.09	.31***	.27***
Oral sex	.14	.08	.02	.03	.00	.16*	.18*
Sex with prostitute	.16	.18*	.17*	.06	.10	.32***	.20*
Gonorrhea	.17*	.19*	.20*	.07	.08	.16*	.21**
Syphilis	.20*	.11	.19*	.20*	.18*	.34***	.53****
Herpes	.17*	.17*	.20*	.20*	.18*	.40****	.47****
Genital warts	.15	.06	.26***	.15#	.17*	.23**	.32***
HIV/AIDS	.19*	.09	.07	.21**	.20*	.37***	.47****

#$p < .10$; *$p < .05$; **$p < .01$; ***$p < .001$; ****$p < .0001$.

standing about the steps that can be taken to reduce AIDS risk, including the identification of high-risk practices, methods to lessen the likelihood of HIV exposure, and common misconceptions about HIV transmission. Finally, the perceived risk of being exposed to the AIDS virus was not significantly associated with the use of either of the drugs.

RELATIONSHIPS BETWEEN DRUG USE, SEXUAL BEHAVIORS, AND ATTITUDES FOR AFRICAN-AMERICAN FEMALES

The major finding that was in direct contrast to the males was the significant association discovered between attitudes about the use of condoms and both smoking cigarettes and drinking (see Table 7.2). However, neither smoking cigarettes nor drinking was significantly associated with the use of condoms. Among the African-American females, smoking was found to be significantly associated with having multiple sex partners and having beliefs about being a member of a AIDS high-risk group. Smoking cigarettes was also significantly associated with the practice of oral sex, having sex with prostitutes, as well as having a history of gonorrhea and herpes. As was the case with the males, the experience of intense angry reactions about the use of condoms was significantly associated with the use of marijuana, crack, and cocaine.

The lack of significant associations between risky sexual behaviors and both crack and cocaine use might be due to the fact that a relatively small percentage of the African-American females reported using these substances, as was the case with PCP where none of the females reported using this substance. Even though a small percentage of females reported using heroin, its use was found to be significantly associated with risky sexual practices (e.g., anal intercourse and having sex with prostitutes) and having a history of sexually transmitted diseases.

PERCEPTIONS OF PERSONAL SUSCEPTIBILITY TO HIV/AIDS INFECTION

In addition to examining the associations of AIDS knowledge and attitudes on sexual behaviors and practices, many of the previously mentioned studies investigated perceptions of vulnerability among adolescent and young adult samples. For example, Strunin and Hingson (1987) report that over half of their sample of 829 teenagers did not worry about contracting AIDS even though they were not consistently practicing safe sex. Similarly, a study conducted by

Table 7.2
Correlations between Drug Use, Sexual Behaviors, and Attitudes for African-American Females

Variables	Smoking	Drinking	Marijuana	Crack	Cocaine	PCP	Heroin
AIDS knowledge	.08	.24**	-.09	-.14#	-.17*	NA	.05
Condom attitudes	.11	.36***	.08	.15#	.10	NA	-.04
Contraceptive	.20**	.29***	.11	.15#	.16#	NA	-.02
Interrupt	.18*	.07	.18*	.11	.15#	NA	-.06
Acceptance	.16*	.36***	.09	.05	.04	NA	-.05
Excitement	.22**	.26***	.13	.10	.11	NA	-.01
Inconvenient	.18*	.07	.14#	.07	.11	NA	.02
Angry reactions	.21**	.17*	.24**	.20**	.19**	NA	-.12
Always use condoms	.01	-.08	.05	.04	.07	NA	-.03
Multiple partners	.25***	.13#	.07	.03	.03	NA	-.01
Four partners in past year	.24**	.12	.06	.03	.02	NA	.00
Perceived risk	-.00	.08	.09	.10	.07	NA	-.08
High risk group	.28***	.08	.05	.00	.02	NA	.12
Anal intercourse	.06	.13#	.02	.00	.04	NA	.28***
Oral sex	.21**	.18*	.14#	.00	.04	NA	.09
Sex with prostitute	.32***	.00	.03	.00	.00	NA	.24**
Gonorrhea	.20**	.00	.05	.05	.06	NA	.29***
Syphilis	.05	.03	.02	.00	.00	NA	.24**
Herpes	.36***	.07	.14#	.00	.01	NA	-.03
Genital warts	.09	.02	.00	.00	.01	NA	.29***
HIV/AIDS	.06	.14#	.09	.07	.08	NA	.23**

#$p < .10$; *$p < .05$; **$p < .01$; ***$p < .001$.

DiClemente and associates (DiClemente, et al., 1987, 1988) revealed that although knowledge about the transmission of AIDS was more than adequate, a greater percentage (54 percent) stated they were not worried about being exposed to HIV/AIDS.

In a study of 374 college students (288 undergraduates, 86 post-graduates), 28 percent of the women and 37 percent of the men were sexually involved with two or three partners, while a little more than one-third (36 percent) of the men and women were sexually involved with three or more partners. Despite the increased risk associated with multiple partnerships, most respondents felt they had a lower than average chance of being exposed to HIV/AIDS than other people of their age group. More specifically, of the 78 percent describing themselves as having lower than average risk, 14 percent had had intercourse with more than three partners (Turner et al., 1988).

A further indication of the low perceived vulnerability in college students is seen in research by Thurman and Franklin (1990) who noted that only 18.3 percent of their sample admitted they felt personally susceptible to the AIDS virus to some extent, with over 44 percent not feeling at all susceptible and less than 36 percent feeling a little susceptible to HIV infection. These low levels of personal susceptibility are intriguing given that over 60 percent feared AIDS would spread throughout the university community.

Baldwin and Baldwin (1988a) compared a number of groups in their perceptions of risk for HIV infection. Their analysis revealed that those who had a new partner in the past three months as compared to those who did not have a new partner were more worried about contracting the disease. Nevertheless, this group reported less caution about sexual encounters and asked their partners fewer questions about past sexual history. Basically, the major finding uncovered by these researchers is that those who engage in casual sex are less likely to use caution and are more worried about contracting AIDS than their counterparts who are in committed relationships.

Interestingly enough, being very knowledgeable about the factors associated with the transmission of AIDS was not significantly related to risky sexual behaviors. In other words, having strong beliefs that you are likely to be exposed to HIV/AIDS does not necessarily motivate people to change their behaviors and adopt safe sex practices. However, the investigators also discovered that 18 percent of those students who worried more than their peers had safer sexual practices.

In another study of adolescent women attending a family planning clinic (Catania, Dolcini, Coates, Kegeles, Greenblatt, Puckett, Corman, and Miller, 1989) it was revealed that having more than one sexual partner was significantly associated with increased susceptibility.

Again, as with Baldwin and Baldwin (1988a), susceptibility findings seem counter-intuitive, with higher levels of perceived risk being associated with high-risk sexual behavior. Thus, one must question the direction assumed in the correlational link between these variables. A study of knowledge about AIDS among adolescent males of varying ethnic groups (Bell, Feraios, and Bryan, 1990) revealed that those who reported "hearing about AIDS" rather than discussing it with others, perceived AIDS to be a problem for others but not for them. In conjunction with this view, those who reported knowing more IV-drug users agreed to statements about AIDS being a problem for others rather than affecting them personally.

In the DiClemente et al. (1987) sample, perceived susceptibility to AIDS scores were calculated ranging from zero (high perceived susceptibility) to three (low perceived susceptibility). Twenty-seven percent, 25 percent, 34 percent, and 14 percent had scores of zero, one, two, and three respectively. In this sample, women saw themselves as more vulnerable to AIDS than men, and Asians reported increased perceptions of risk more often than other ethnic groups.

The results of research using black and Hispanic female adolescents were consistent with these findings. This research indicates that only 7.2 percent of the sample worried "often," and 9.9 percent were worried "all the time" about getting AIDS. Even though 61.2 percent worried sometimes, and 21.6 percent never worried, risky sexual practices were very prevalent in this group, with 54.6 percent reporting they did not change their sexual behaviors to avoid AIDS. Although the level of worry is apparently low in this sample, reported change in sexual practices was significantly correlated with level of worry, suggesting that perceived vulnerability may facilitate self-protective behaviors (Jaffe et al., 1988). Consistent with these findings, Ishii-Kuntz (1988) found that feelings of personal concern about contracting AIDS among University of California students were strongly associated with perceived behavior changes. Those who were more concerned with AIDS were more likely to use condoms, less likely to engage in unprotected oral and anal sex, increase the length of time before intercourse, and question their potential sexual partners about their past sexual history.

Overall, the interpretations of the research in this area are somewhat inconclusive. The findings from several studies indicate that the association between susceptibility of being exposed to HIV/AIDS and risky sexual behavior is a positive one. In other words, individuals who believe that they are at increased risk of being exposed to HIV/AIDS are more likely to engage in risky sexual practices. While I have no way of knowing the real reasons for this effect, it is possible that individuals who engage in unsafe and risky sexual practices are more aware of the risks of acquiring AIDS via sex and thus worry more. It should also be noted that the information obtained from most studies is correlational in nature and that it is possible that worries about AIDS followed rather than preceded sexual behaviors. However, without longitudinal follow-up studies, one cannot be certain if in fact the reverse is true. In any case, there tends to be a large gap between the perception of risk and risky sexual behavior. Much like the studies of the association between knowledge about AIDS and risky sexual behaviors, which were found to be very poor, it appears that risky sexual behaviors are not consistently associated with having strong beliefs and fears about being exposed to HIV/AIDS.

Before turning to the findings for individuals who at are extreme risk, I want to describe the perception of risk for the African-American subjects in the present inquiry. The findings are somewhat restrictive and focused on responses to six items that tap into the perception of risk. Basically, there was no significant difference ($x^2 = .11$) in the percentage of African-American males (80 percent) and females (77 percent) who reported that they were "afraid of getting AIDS." However, a significantly larger ($x^2 = 6.61$, $p < .01$) percentage of African-American males (40 percent) than females (27 percent) reported that they were "not worried about getting AIDS." A significantly larger ($x^2 = 6.69$, $p < .01$) percentage of males (55 percent) than females (38 percent) also believe that they are "less likely than most people to get AIDS." However, there was no significant difference in the percentage of males (54 percent) and females (48 percent) who believed that they were "not the kind of person who is likely to get AIDS." There was also a relatively large percentage of males and females (77 percent for both groups) who reported that they "would rather get any other disease than AIDS." Finally, a significantly larger percentage of African-American males (16 percent) than females (10 percent) consider themselves a member of the AIDS "high-risk group."

INDIVIDUALS AT EXTREME RISK OF BEING EXPOSED TO HIV/AIDS

In order to examine the associations between the extreme personal beliefs about the risk of being exposed to HIV/AIDS and risky sexual behaviors, subjects were divided into three Perceived Risk Groups (Low, Moderate, and High) based on a split of the distribution of scores on the "Perceived Risk Scale" in approximately equal thirds. The Perceived Risk Scale was formed by summing the responses to the individual items that are described in the methodology section in Chapter 2. The data for males and females were combined in the analyses conducted for this section. The Perceived Risk scores and the number of subjects in each group were: 1–2 ($n = 97$); 3–4 ($n = $

Table 7.3
AIDS Knowledge, Attitudes about Using Condoms as a Function of Low, Moderate, and High Perceptions of Risk of Getting AIDS

Variables	Low (N=97) Mean	SD	Mod. (N=116) Mean	SD	High (N=111) Mean	SD	F-Tests
AIDS knowledge	23.5	4.6	23.7	4.6	23.6	4.1	.05
Condom attitudes	32.3	8.8	31.8	10.4	32.2	8.6	.08
Contraceptive	14.6	4.1	15.4	3.9	14.9	3.9	.87
Inconvenient	6.8	3.0	7.6	3.8	7.7	3.1	1.73
Excites	11.2	3.5	11.6	3.4	11.0	3.1	.80
Interrupts	15.0	5.2	15.1	6.4	15.7	5.3	.37
Acceptance	17.0	3.9	17.0	4.2	17.3	3.9	.15
Angry Reactions	18.2	7.5	17.7	6.8	17.9	7.4	.10
Smoking	1.4	1.0	1.4	1.2	1.5	1.2	.23
Drinking	2.4	1.3	2.5	1.3	2.8	1.4	2.09
Marijuana	1.3	1.1	1.3	1.1	1.4	1.1	.20
Crack	1.1	.8	1.0	.7	1.1	.7	.40
Cocaine	1.1	.8	1.0	.7	1.1	.8	.48

106); 5–6 ($n = 111$). Three-way analyses of variance were used to compare the average scores on the AIDS Knowledge Questionnaire and Condom Attitude Questionnaire. The measures of drug use (cigarette, marijuana, crack, cocaine) were treated as continuous variables (i.e., low-to-high usage) and the average scores were also compared using three-way analyses of variance techniques (see Table 7.3). In general, the results of the analyses did not reveal any significant differences between the three Perceived Risk Groups.

Additional comparisons using chi-square analyses were conducted to determine whether subjects in the three Perceived Risk Groups differed from each other with regard to their involvement in risky sexual behaviors and previous treatment for sexually transmitted diseases (see Table 7.4). An observation of the data presented in the bottom part of Table 7.4 shows that the three groups differed from each other in the percentage of people who practiced oral sex and who had multiple sex partners. Basically, the pattern of these findings show that a significantly larger percentage of individuals in the High Perceived Risk Group participate in oral sex and have multiple sex partners. The three groups did not differ with regard to the percentage of subjects who had been previously treated for STDs or HIV/AIDS. Finally, a significantly larger percentage of subjects in the High Perceived Risk Group believe they are a member of the AIDS high-risk group.

Table 7.4
Risky Sexual Behaviors as a Function of Low, Moderate, and High Perceptions of Risk of Getting AIDS

Variables	Low %	Moderate %	High %	Chi-Square
Anal intercourse	12	14	19	1.48
Oral sex	30	47	48	7.34*
Gonorrhea	8	11	13	1.11
Syphilis	3	4	5	1.04
Herpes	4	4	3	3.25
Genital warts	1	5	8	4.26
Condoms should be used	77	81	86	2.28
Always use condoms	27	27	36	2.31
Sex with prostitute	5	9	13	2.99
HIV/AIDS	7	3	5	1.68
Four or more partners	24	31	43	7.14*
High risk AIDS group	1	6	19	16.82****

*$p < .05$; ****$p < .0001$.

The last set of analyses took a different approach to looking at the relationship between "risk" and behavior. In these analyses, subjects were assigned to one of three groups according to the presence of the following five risky sexual behaviors: (1) anal intercourse, (2) never using condoms, (3) being sexually involved with four or more partners, (4) experiencing sex with prostitutes, and (5) having a history of sexually transmitted diseases. For this sample, there were no subjects who did not engage in either of the five risky sexual behaviors. For purposes of analyses, subjects assigned to Group-1 had only one of the risk factors, while subjects in Group-2 had two of the risk factors. Subjects assiged to Group-3 had three or more of the five risk factors and are considered to be at "highest risk" for being exposed to HIV/AIDS. The data presented in Table 7.5 shows that the three groups were not significantly different from each other in their knowledge about factors responsible for the transmission of HIV/AIDS. However, the groups were found to have significantly different attitudes about the use of condoms.

As can be observed, the attitudes about the use of condoms were significantly more negative for subjects in Group-3. This was true for the total scale score of the Condom Attitudes Questionnaire ($F = 3.47$, $p < .05$) and two subscales that assessed whether condoms were Inconvenient ($F = 25.75$, $p < .0001$) and caused Interruptions during

Table 7.5
Extreme Risk of AIDS — I: Individuals with One, Two, and Three or More Risk Factors for HIV/AIDS

	1 Risk Factor		2 Risk Factors		3 Risk Factors[a]		
Variables	Mean	SD	Mean	SD	Mean	SD	F-Tests
AIDS knowledge	23.5	4.8	22.8	4.9	22.6	5.5	.87
Condom attitudes	31.8	10.3	31.2	8.1	37.6	6.9	3.47*
Contraceptive	14.7	4.6	15.4	3.5	15.5	3.5	.92
Inconvenient	6.7	3.1	8.3	3.1	10.6	3.4	25.75****
Excites	10.9	3.7	11.2	2.8	11.6	2.8	.78
Interrupts	14.6	5.6	16.5	5.5	19.8	4.6	15.33****
Acceptable	16.8	4.7	17.5	3.6	16.1	3.3	1.47
Angry reactions	17.3	6.9	18.9	6.1	20.9	7.3	5.04***
Smoking	1.3	.9	1.5	1.2	1.9	1.8	3.32*
Drinking	2.4	1.2	2.7	1.4	3.1	1.6	4.91***
Marijuana	1.3	1.3	1.4	.9	1.9	1.6	3.13*
Crack	1.1	1.1	1.0	.4	1.2	1.1	.52
Cocaine	1.1	1.1	1.1	.6	1.3	1.1	.36
Perceived risk	3.0	1.1	3.1	1.2	3.5	.9	2.49

$*p < .05; **p < .01; ***p < .001; ****p < .0001.$
[a]or more

foreplay and sex $(F = 15.33, p < .0001)$. Interestingly enough, the three groups did not differ with regard to their attitudes about the use of condoms as a contraceptive. Another important finding was that subjects in Group-3 reported that they experience angry reactions about the negotiation of condoms more intensely than subjects in the other groups. The subjects in Group-3 also reported greater use of cigarettes, alcohol, and marijuana. However, there was no significant difference in the use of crack or cocaine for the three groups. Additional analyses were conducted in order to take a closer look at the profile of risk factors for each of the three groups (see Table 7.6). As can be observed, a significantly larger percentage of subjects in Group-3 engaged in anal intercourse (69 percent), oral-genital sex (91 percent), experienced sex with prostitutes (60 percent), and have been involved with four or more partners in the past year (86 percent). Similarly, a significantly larger percentage of subjects in Group-3 have been treated for gonorrhea (58 percent), syphilis (16 percent), herpes (18 percent), and genital warts (27 percent). Whereas the three groups did not differ in their beliefs about the use of condoms, a significantly larger percentage of subjects in Group-3 have HIV/AIDS (14 percent) compared to subjects in Group-1 (2 percent) and Group-2 (7 percent) which constituted the groups at lower risk.

Table 7.6
Extreme Risk of AIDS—II: Individuals with One, Two, and Three or More Risk Factors for HIV/AIDS

Variables	1 Risk Factor		2 Risk Factors		3 Risk Factors[a]		Chi-Square
	%	N	%	N	%	N	
Anal sex	3	4	16	10	69	31	95.27****
Oral sex	26	34	64	39	91	39	64.47****
Gonorrhea	1	2	8	5	58	26	93.50****
Syphilis	0	0	10	6	16	7	19.11***
Herpes	1	2	3	2	18	8	24.36***
Genital warts	1	2	5	3	27	12	33.89***
Condoms should be used	79	102	81	44	65	24	4.03
Always use condoms	19	25	13	8	18	8	1.11
Sex with prostitutes	0	0	3	2	60	27	119.57****
HIV/AIDS	2	3	7	4	14	6	8.54**
Four partners	14	18	77	46	86	36	105.60****
High risk AIDS group	3	4	14	8	33	13	29.05***

$**p < .01$; $***p < .001$; $****p < .0001$.
[a]or more

The most puzzling finding was the lack of any significant difference in the perception of risk for subjects in the three groups. The overall pattern of the findings for this set of analyses indicates that African-American males and females who engage in high-risk sexual behaviors tend to believe that they are not at risk for being exposed to HIV/AIDS. They are basically not worried and they do not consider themselves to be the kind of person to get AIDS—even though they are engaging in sexual behaviors that increase the probability of exposure to the AIDS virus. There is no doubt that a significant proportion of this sample, even though they engage in risky sexual behaviors, are not yet exposed to HIV. It may be the case that one of the reasons for the lack of association between risky behaviors and the perception of risk is that individuals who have engaged in past high-risk behaviors believe that HIV exposure has probably already taken place and behavior change is less important.

In summary, the interrelationships between drug use, risky sexual behaviors, and perceived risk of being exposed to AIDS are complex for African-Americans and somewhat different for males and females. For males, it appears that "recreational drugs" such as cigarettes, alcohol, marijuana, and cocaine/crack are significantly associated with several of the risky sexual behaviors and having the AIDS virus.

However, the use of these drugs was not significantly associated with knowledge about AIDS or the perceived susceptibility of being exposed to the AIDS virus. The exceptions were the use of PCP and heroin. Even so, the most troublesome finding for the males was the fact that both PCP and heroin were strongly associated with risky sexual behaviors, having a history of STDs, and having HIV/AIDS. To a certain extent, a history of heroin use was also significantly related to risky sexual practices and histories of STDs among African-American females. However, the relationships were not as strong as those discovered for males. Among the females, cigarette smoking was found to be most consistently associated with risky sexual behaviors and having a history of STDs. There was no significant relationship between the use of drugs and the perceived risk of getting HIV/AIDS. Of most importance are the results which show that there is no significant relationship between risky sexual behaviors and the perceived risk of being exposed to the AIDS virus.

CHAPTER 8

Anal Intercourse among African-American Heterosexuals

There remains very little doubt that anal intercourse, particularly receptive anal intercourse, is one of the most significant factors that predict HIV infection and AIDS (Darrow, Jaffe, and Curran, 1983; Blattner, Biggar, Weiss, Melbye, and Goedert, 1985; Winkelstein, Lyman, Padin, et al., 1987; Detels, Visscher, Kingsley, and Chimel, 1987). Most studies show that being on the receiving end of anal intercourse carries the greatest risk for both heterosexuals and gays. From a physiological perspective, blood vessels in tissue lining the anus and rectum are easily ruptured and torn because of the trauma that often accompanies this activity. These ruptures and tears permit semen-borne HIV to have a direct passageway to the bloodstream. As indicated earlier, most studies show the receptive partner to be at greater risk of being exposed to HIV. However, the insertive partner may also be exposed to the virus via contact with the partner's blood or body fluids.

Anal intercourse may be one of the most efficient modes of male-to-female heterosexual transmission of HIV among African-Americans and other ethnic groups, but very little is known about this sexual practice among African-Americans. The purpose of this chapter is to describe information concerning the prevalence of the practice of anal intercourse for the sample of African-American college students. Information concerning the relationships between anal intercourse and knowledge about AIDS, attitudes about the use of condoms, drug use, perceived risk of being exposed to HIV/AIDS, STDs, and other risky sexual behaviors are described.

HOW PREVALENT IS THE PRACTICE OF
ANAL INTERCOURSE AMONG AFRICAN-AMERICANS?

The exact figures are a bit difficult to come up with, although anal intercourse is a common sexual practice among heterosexuals. A major reason that contributes to the lack of information concerning anal intercourse is that for many ethnic groups sexual intercourse is considered to be inclusive of "vaginal sex" only. In this case, all heterosexual activities other than vaginal intercourse are considered to be part of foreplay (Martin, 1990; Luria, Friedman, and Rose, 1987). Another reason may be that there is a very strong societal taboo associated with the discussion of anal sex. For example, even in Kinsey's seminal work on human sexual behaviors, there were no survey questions about the practice of anal intercourse (Kinsey et al., 1953). Nevertheless, information derived from studies where the sample sizes are relatively small indicate that from 6 to 60 percent of adults have experienced anal sex. These studies have included such a small sample of African-Americans that it is impossible to accurately indicate the prevalence of this sexual act.

Anal intercourse is assumed to be very common among gay males, but infrequently practiced among heterosexuals. In some studies (Hunt, 1974; Luria, Friedman, and Rose, 1987; Tarvis and Sands, 1975), anal intercourse has been tried once or twice by 25 to 45 percent of heterosexual couples. In a study reported by Reinisch, Sanders, and Ziemba-Davis (1988), approximately 18 percent of self-identified heterosexual males reported having engaged in anal sex. The data for women revealed that 39 percent reported having at least one experience with anal intercourse. One prevalence study of 526 consecutive gynecologic patients found that anal intecourse was an incidental practice for 25 percent and a regular means of sexual gratification for 8 percent of the sample. Interestingly enough, none of the patients who engaged in anal sex had any symptoms or diagnostic signs resulting from anal intercourse (Bolling, 1977).

RESULTS FOR THE COLLEGE SAMPLE

The findings for the sample of African-American college students revealed that 13 percent of the males and 9 percent of the females reported having experienced anal intercourse. Among the males, anal intercourse was significantly associated with sexually transmitted diseases such as gonorrhea ($r = .34$, $p < .01$), genital warts ($r = .52$, $p < .0001$), and HIV/AIDS ($r = .42$, $p < .0001$). Not all experiences with anal intercourse included male partners, as reflected by

Table 8.1
Correlations between Anal Intercourse, STDs, Drug Use, and Sexual Behaviors

Variables	Males	Females
Gonorrhea	.34**	.26**
Syphilis	.15#	.12
Herpes	.08	.47***
Genital warts	.52***	.36**
HIV/AIDS	.46***	.39***
Sex with male	.57***	.97****
Four or more partners in past year	.19*	.28**
Sex with prostitute	.22*	.11
Always used condoms	-.12	.16
Cigarettes	.01	.34**
Alcohol	.08	.12
Marijuana	-.05	.06
Crack	.05	.11
Cocaine	-.08	.14

$\#p < .10$; $*p < .05$; $**p < .01$; $***p < .001$; $****p < .0001$.

the significant correlation of $r = .57$ ($p < .0001$) between anal intercourse and having sex with males (see Table 8.1). The reported experience of anal intercourse was not found to be significantly related to drug use, but was significantly associated with having multiple sex partners ($r = .19$, $p < .05$), and experiencing sex with prostitutes ($r = .22$, $p < .05$). However, the practice of anal sex was not significantly associated with the consistent use ("always use") of condoms for males.

Among the African-American females, anal intercourse was significantly correlated with gonorrhea ($r = .26$, $p < .01$), genital warts ($r = .36$, $p < .01$), and having HIV/AIDS ($r = .39$, $p < .001$). As might be expected, nearly all of the women under discussion experienced anal intercourse with males as evidenced by the relatively large and significant correlation between the experience of anal intercourse and having sex with males ($r = .97$, $p < .0001$). Much like the results for males, the experience of anal sex was unrelated to drug use; the one exception was the significant relationship observed between

Table 8.2
Characteristics of Individuals Who Engage in Anal Intercourse—I

Variables	YES	SD	NO	SD	T-Tests
AIDS knowledge	22.8	5.1	23.5	4.9	.81
Perceived risk	3.3	1.0	3.1	1.0	.89
Condom attitudes	32.4	9.6	28.7	8.3	2.68**
Contraceptive	15.6	3.1	14.9	4.2	1.32
Interrupts	18.8	5.3	14.7	5.7	4.59****
Acceptable	16.5	3.3	17.1	34.3	1.04
Excites	11.6	2.3	11.2	3.5	1.06
Inconvenient	9.8	3.8	7.0	3.2	4.54****
Angry reactions	21.1	6.3	17.3	7.2	3.59****
Smoking	1.6	1.7	1.4	1.1	.79
Drinking	2.7	1.4	2.5	1.3	.91
Marijuana	1.6	1.5	1.3	1.06	1.06
Crack	1.2	1.1	1.1	.8	.61
Cocaine	1.3	1.1	1.1	.8	.13

*$p < .05$; **$p < .01$; ***$p < .001$; ****$p < .0001$.

anal sex and cigarette smoking ($r = .34$, $p < .01$). As was the case for males, the experience of anal sex was signficantly correlated with having four or more partners ($r = .28$, $p < .01$).

In order to get a better understanding of the variables related to anal intercourse in this sample, analyses were conducted to determine those variables that significantly discriminate between those individuals who practice anal sex from those who do not. Data for males and females were combined in all analyses. The outcome of these analyses are presented in Table 8.2. As can be observed, there was no significant difference in knowledge about AIDS, drug use, or the perceived susceptibility of being exposed to the AIDS virus. Whereas the two groups did not differ in the extent to which condoms are always used during sex, subjects who engaged in anal sex have significantly more negative attitudes about the use of condoms and they report becoming more intensely angered about the negotiation of using condoms with their partner.

The data presented in Table 8.3 show that a significantly (all x^2 analyses were significant at $p < .0001$) larger percentage of subjects

Table 8.3
Characteristics of Individuals Who Engage in Anal Intercourse—II

Variables	YES (%)	NO (%)	Chi-Square
Oral sex	82	36	32.44****
Sex with prostitutes	40	4	55.78****
Four or more partners	61	29	15.88****
Condoms should be used during sex	65	83	7.03
Always use condoms	30	30	.01
Gonorrhea	38	6	39.96****
Syphilis	11	3	6.07**
Herpes	9	3	4.39*
Genital warts	24	2	35.72****
HIV/AIDS	12	3	6.77**
High risk AIDS group	21	8	6.51

$*p < .05; **p < .01; ***p < .001; ****p < .0001.$

who practice anal intercourse compared to those who do not also engage in oral-genital sex (82 percent versus 36 percent), have multiple sex partners (61 percent versus 29 percent), and have sex with prostitutes (40 percent versus 4 percent). In general, the prevalence of sexually transmitted diseases was between 3-to-10 times higher among subjects who engaged in anal sex. The information presented in Table 8.3 also reveals that a significantly larger percentage of subjects who engaged in anal sex indicated that they believe that they are in a "high-risk" AIDS groups (21 percent versus 8 percent). Finally, the percentage of subjects with HIV/AIDS was significantly higher among subjects who engaged in anal intercourse (12 percent) compared to those individuals who did not (3 percent).

The data for the sample of African-American college males and females clearly show that the practice of anal intercourse is significantly related to STDs and to having HIV/AIDS for both males and females. For the most part, the magnitude of the correlations between anal sex and STDs (including HIV/AIDS) were very similar for males and females. Therefore, the risk of HIV infection and exposure to STDs associated with anal intercourse appears to be very similar for African-American males and females. One of the limitations of the assessment of anal intercourse is that it does not distinguish between insertive and receptive intercourse. Because of this it is not possible to fully determine whether the HIV risk-profile is worse for subjects who are on the receiving end of anal intercourse. In the case of the African-American women in this sample, they are all on the receiving end and the risk of being exposed to HIV/AIDS and STDs appears to be the same for women as it is for men in this sample.

One of the most troubling results uncovered about the practice of anal sex is that so few of the African-American subjects who engage in the practice use condoms (30 percent), yet a relatively large percentage of these subjects (65 percent) believe that condoms "should" be used during intercourse. Furthermore, they are well aware of the health risks associated with the practice of unprotected anal sex as evident by their responses to the AIDS knowledge questionnaire.

Condom use has been widely advocated as a protection against HIV transmission during anal intercourse. While the most encouragement has been directed toward men who practice anal sex to use condoms, the findings from this study indicate that condom use during anal sex is a realistic way for African-American women to avoid HIV infection. Several in vitro studies have indicated that latex condoms provide an effective barrier to HIV-transmission and that the virus becomes partially inactivated inside the condom, particularly when used in conjunction with spermicides or lubricants containing nonoxynol-9 (Rietmeijer, Krebs, Feorino, and Judson, 1987; Scesney, Gantz, and Sullivan, 1987; Feldblum and Fortney, 1988; Van de Perre, Jacobs, and Sprecher-Goldberger, 1987). There is little doubt that condoms can be an effective barrier to HIV infection. For example, a recent prospective study by Detels et al. (1989) revealed that condom use is a significant, but not foolproof, method of protection against being exposed to the AIDS virus. The major findings revealed in this study indicate that gay men who used condoms only some of the time were six times more likely to become infected with the AIDS virus than gay men who used condoms all the time. Even among individuals who use condoms all the time there is a possibility that during intercourse condoms can break or slip off. Be this as it may, important questions about how to effectively encourage African-Americans to use condoms still remain unanswered. It is my belief that the answers can be found, but we will need to invest as much attention to this problem as we have invested in marketing and advertising certain brands of cigarettes, liquors, and athletic shoes to the African-American public.

When I first started this project I strongly believed that "increasing knowledge" about the causes, consequences, and prevention of the AIDS virus among African-Americans would sufficiently alter the source of the epidemic among this group of people. I can sadly say that I was wrong. At least for the time being, the AIDS educational campaign may not be reaching young African-American adults in a way that motivates them to make changes in their sexual behaviors. The fact that the data from which I base this conclusion is derived from college students makes it a bit more difficult to believe that the AIDS educational efforts have affected African-Americans. In other words, if the African-American college students, who are the best and brightest—the cream of the crop—knowingly engage in sexual behaviors that increase the risk of exposure to the AIDS virus, then individuals who are less fortunate and not as well educated are possibly more likely to be engaging in behaviors that place themselves at greater risk for HIV exposure. While this is a frightening possibility, the solution for slowing the AIDS and STD epidemics might be targeting younger age groups who have not yet engaged in sexual intercourse.

Today as I begin the second phase of my research with African-American college students, I find myself again feeling optimistic about the prevention of HIV/AIDS. The major spark for my optimistic attitude is that a well-known, respected, and recognized African-American (Magic Johnson) public figure has come forth to describe his problems with the HIV virus. There is no doubt that Magic Johnson will serve as a credible model and encourage standards of conduct which will demonstrate to others that it is important to protect oneself from exposure to HIV. Nevertheless, his message may have nothing more than a short-term impact, if that, on African-Americans. Even this short-term effect is likely to entail a shift in attitudes without any apparent effect on risky sexual behaviors. While my opinion on this matter may appear to be a bit cynical and negative, one has only to consider the notably small influence professional African-American athlete role models have had on other significant problems (e.g., drug abuse, teenage pregnancy, programs to encourage youth to stay in school) to realize that the odds do not favor a significant impact.

CHAPTER 9

Characteristics of African-American College Students with HIV/AIDS

This chapter will identify the factors that are significantly associated to HIV/AIDS among the sample of African-American college students. First of all, being male was significantly associated with having HIV/AIDS. In other words, a significantly larger percentage of African-American males (6.5 percent) than females (2 percent) have HIV/AIDS. Of the individuals with HIV/AIDS, 69 percent were males and 31 percent were females. This pattern tends to be consistent with results obtained from epidemiological studies of the prevalence of HIV/AIDS among adults throughout the United States.

Before describing other results, it is important to understand how the data for this chapter are organized. Obviously, very few of the African-American college students have HIV/AIDS, and the numbers are too small to conduct meaningful analyses separately for males and females. Therefore, one of the logical things to do is to combine the data for males and females into a single analysis. The problem with this approach is that important information about differences between males and females could be overlooked. Another solution is to conduct preliminary analyses to determine if there are significant differences between males and females with HIV/AIDS, and if none are found, then the data can be combined and the conclusions derived from the findings will apply equally to males and females. This last approach to handling the data was the one selected for organizing the information in this chapter. The preliminary analyses did not reveal any statistically significant differences in the sexual behaviors and attitudes of the African-American males and females with HIV/AIDS. The basic strategy for the analyses is to compare the group with HIV/AIDS to subjects without HIV/AIDS on variables that have

Table 9.1
Characteristics of Individuals with HIV/AIDS—I

Variables	+HIV/AIDS		-HIV/AIDS		
	Mean	SD	Mean	SD	F-Tests
AIDS knowledge	16.4	9.2	24.3	3.7	3.10**
Perceived risk	2.9	1.3	3.0	1.1	.34
Condom attitudes-total	28.9	10.5	32.4	8.9	1.13
Contraceptive	14.3	6.9	15.1	3.7	.40
Interrupts	16.8	7.6	15.3	5.2	-.68
Acceptance	15.8	6.5	17.3	3.7	.82
Excites	11.8	5.0	11.5	3.1	-.25
Inconvenient	7.3	3.7	7.4	3.2	.09
Angry reactions	21.1	12.4	17.0	6.6	-1.13
Smoking	1.76	1.9	1.66	1.5	-.19
Drinking	2.69	2.5	2.78	1.3	.12
Crack	1.62	1.9	1.03	.7	-1.05
Cocaine	1.61	1.9	1.14	.8	-.86

$**p < .01$.

been discussed throughout the book. For comparison purposes, subjects without HIV/AIDS will be referred to as the NO-HIV/AIDS group, while subjects with HIV/AIDS will be referred to as the YES-HIV/AIDS group.

KNOWLEDGE ABOUT AIDS AND PERCEIVED RISK
OF EXPOSURE TO HIV/AIDS

The first question to be examined was whether knowledge about factors associated with the transmission of HIV/AIDS is lower for subjects in the YES-HIV/AIDS group compared to subjects without HIV/AIDS. Based on the information about the association (lack of) between knowledge and risky sexual behaviors that have been discussed throughout the book, my best guess is that there would be no significant relationship between the level of knowledge about factors associated with the transmission of HIV/AIDS and actually having HIV/AIDS. To my surprise, however, the AIDS Knowledge Questionnaire scores for subjects in the YES-HIV/AIDS group (16.4 +

Table 9.2
Characteristics of Individuals with HIV/AIDS – II

Variables	+HIV (%)	-HIV (%)	Chi-Square
Anal intercourse	42	15	6.17**
Oral sex	67	50	1.25
Sex with prostitute	54	7	37.13****
Four or more partners	38	33	.19
Gonorrhea	38	8	15.18***
Syphilis	38	2	58.87****
Herpes	31	3	30.04****
Genital warts	38	4	30.16****
Condoms should be used	77	81	2.28
Always use condoms	85	27	20.61****
Condoms not necessary if you love your partner	38	17	7.28**

$**p < .01$; $***p < .001$; $****p < .0001$.

9.2) were significantly lower than those of subjects without HIV/AIDS (24.3 + 3.7), as reflected by the comparison made using a t-test ($t =$ 3.10, p < .009). More specifically, the YES-HIV/AIDS group correctly answered 55 percent of the AIDS knowledge questions, while the subjects without HIV/AIDS correctly answered 85 percent of the questions (see Tables 9.1 and 9.2). So, while across the board AIDS knowledge was unrelated to risky sexual behaviors, having a lower level of knowledge about AIDS was significantly related to having acquired HIV/AIDS.

The questions that were problematic for the subjects with HIV/ AIDS were quite varied. For example, even though a large percentage of subjects with HIV/AIDS knew that "stress does not cause AIDS" (Question #3), approximately 11 percent believed that stress causes AIDS compared to 1 percent of the subjects without HIV/AIDS. A significantly smaller percentage of the subjects in the YES-HIV/AIDS group compared to the NO-HIV/AIDS group correctly responded to questions about whether you can get AIDS from kissing (Question #4; 89 percent versus 99 percent) or touching someone with AIDS (Question #5; 88 percent versus 98 percent). A substantially lower percentage of subjects with HIV/AIDS (71 percent) correctly responded to the question about whether all gay men have AIDS (Question #6) compared to 94 percent of the subjects without HIV/AIDS. AIDS is believed to be "not at all serious, like having a cold" (Question #11) by 20 percent of the subjects with HIV/AIDS compared to 4 percent of the subjects in the NO-HIV/AIDS group.

In addition to the problems above, the AIDS knowledge deficits of the subjects in the YES-HIV/AIDS group extended to several major variables that are directly associated with the transmission of the AIDS virus. For example, only 80 percent of the subjects with HIV/AIDS compared to 96 percent of the subjects in the NO-HIV/AIDS group reported knowing that "having sex with someone who has AIDS is one way of getting the disease" (Question #16). Similarly, a substantially lower percentage of subjects in the YES-HIV/AIDS group reported knowing that "using a condom during sex lowers the risk of getting AIDS" (Question #19) (70 percent for YES versus 97 percent for the NO-HIV/AIDS group). The subjects with HIV/AIDS also exhibited significant knowledge deficits on questions about someone with AIDS "receiving a blood transfusion with infected blood" (Question #2), and "sharing a needle with a drug user who has the disease" (Question #22). Finally, a significantly larger percentage of subjects with HIV/AIDS than subjects without believe that "you can avoid getting AIDS by exercising regularly" (Question #27) (15 percent versus 3 percent, respectively). Similarly, a larger percentage of subjects with HIV/AIDS than subjects in the NO-HIV/AIDS group believe that "AIDS can be cured if treated early" (Question #28) (18 percent versus 5 percent, respectively). Interestingly, there were no significant differences between the two groups in their perceived susceptibility of getting AIDS, as reflected by the scores on the Perceived Risk Scale (mean score 2.9 + 1.3 for the YES group and 3.0 + 1.1 for the NO-HIV/AIDS group).

In summary, African-American college students who reported having HIV/AIDS exhibit several deficits in their knowledge about the factors associated with the transmission and treatment of AIDS. Even though it may be that some of the deficits are a reaction to having been exposed to the AIDS virus, certain deficit areas are more likely to have been associated with exposure to the AIDS virus. For example, the responses to questions 16 (Having sex with someone who has AIDS is one way of getting the disease), 19 (Using a condom during sex can lower the risk of getting AIDS), and 22 (You can get AIDS by sharing a needle with a drug user who has the disease) indicate that between 10 and 30 percent of the subjects with HIV/AIDS were unaware of the risk associated with these behaviors. Therefore, it is highly probable that the AIDS knowledge deficits may have contributed to the risky sexual behaviors and the subsequent exposure to HIV/AIDS.

ATTITUDES ABOUT THE USE OF CONDOMS

The second major area that was examined was the attitudes about the use of condoms for subjects with and without HIV/AIDS. In general, the subjects with HIV/AIDS had very similar attitudes about the use of condoms compared with subjects without HIV/AIDS. Both groups had similar views about the use of condoms as contraceptives and the degree to which condoms were interruptive and inconvenient during foreplay and sexual intercourse. Even though subjects with HIV/AIDS had a higher level of negative attitudes about the general acceptance of condoms than subjects in the NO-HIV/AIDS group, the differences between the mean scores on this scale were not statistically significant. By comparison, a significantly larger percentage of subject in the YES-HIV/AIDS group (38 percent) compared to the NO-HIV/AIDS group (17 percent) believed that "condoms are not necessary if you love your partner." Similarly, a significantly larger percentage of subjects with HIV/AIDS (85 percent) compared to subjects without the disease (27 percent) reported that they "always use condoms."

Given the fact that on average approximately one-third of the sample of African-American students reported that they "always use condoms," the relatively larger percentage of subjects with HIV/AIDS who use condoms (85 percent) is likely to reflect a change in condom use following exposure to the AIDS virus. This latter finding is consistent with previous research (Fox, Ostrow, Valdiserri, Van Radden, Visscher, and Polk, 1987; Joseph, Montgomery, Kessler, Ostrow, Emmons, and Phair, 1987; Coates, Morin, and McKusick, 1987; Willoughby, Schechter, Boyko, Craib, Weaver, and Douglas, 1987) which indicates reductions in risk behavior (i.e., greater use of condoms) among individuals after learning they have the AIDS virus. While it is a good thing for subjects with HIV/AIDS to always use condoms with their partners, there is no way of knowing if condoms were used immediately after finding out about the HIV/AIDS infection or if there was a lengthy delay. There is also a remote possibility that subjects with HIV/AIDS may be responding to the questions concerning the use of condoms in a "socially desirable" manner. In other words, they may be simply saying that they always use condoms. Even if it is true that condoms are always being used by these individuals, there is no guarantee or certainty that they will continue to use condoms in the future or with a new partner. To a great extent, it is my belief that the continuous use of condoms will be determined in part by whether the other partner is aware of the HIV/AIDS infection.

Unfortunately, most of the studies of risk reductions among individuals diagnosed with the AIDS virus have been conducted on gay and bisexual men, most of whom are white. With this as a factor that limits the generalization of the finding, the results from most of the studies consistently show that approximately 75 percent of gay and bisexual males attempt to change their behavior by reducing the number of sexual partners and sexual practices they participate in that facilitate the transmission of HIV/AIDS (Joseph et al., 1987; McKusick et al., 1987; McKusick et al., 1988; Nyanjom, Greaves, Delapenha, Barnes, Boynes, and Frederick, 1987). There is an obvious need to learn more about the changes in risky sexual behaviors among heterosexuals after they find out they have the AIDS virus. Even though there are existing studies of this issue among heterosexuals (Alter, Francis, et al., 1987; Flynn, Jain, Harper, Bailey, Anderson, and Acuna, 1987; Kegels, Catania, and Coates, 1987), very few African-American subjects have been included in these studies and no attempts have been made to determine whether the changes observed for whites are similar to those observed for African-Americans. Nevertheless, the findings of the existing studies have generally revealed that heterosexuals with multiple sexual partners make fewer spontaneous changes in their sexual behaviors than gay or bisexual males (Alter, Francis, et al., 1987; Flynn et al., 1987; Kegels, Catania, and Coates, 1987). As I indicated earlier, most of these previous studies have not included African-American subjects. Therefore, it is not certain whether findings observed in previous research are generalizable to African-American populations.

DRUG USE

The third major set of variables to be examined consisted of recreational drug use. There were no significant differences between the two groups in the use of cigarettes or marijuana. In contrast to this observation, a significantly larger percentage of subjects in the NO-HIV/AIDS group (80 percent) reported using alcohol compared to subjects with HIV/AIDS (38 percent). This finding was unexpected and the opposite of what I had predicted. On the other hand, the results for cocaine and crack use were directly in line with what was predicted. A significantly larger percentage of subjects with HIV/AIDS (25 percent) reported using cocaine and crack compared to 2 percent and 10 percent of the subjects without HIV/AIDS. Finally, a significantly larger percentage of subjects with HIV/AIDS reported having used PCP (26 percent versus 7 percent) and heroin (13 percent versus 0 percent) in the past.

SEXUAL BEHAVIORS AND SEXUALLY TRANSMITTED DISEASES

The final set of variables that were examined consisted of certain sexual behaviors that are considered to be risky and the histories of sexually transmitted diseases. As Table 9.2 shows, subjects with HIV/AIDS were about three times more likely than subjects in the NO-HIV/AIDS group to practice anal intercourse and seven times as likely to report having engaged in sex with prostitutes. There was a tendency for a larger percentage of subjects with HIV/AIDS to practice oral-genital sex (67 percent) compared to the subjects without HIV/AIDS (50 percent), but these differences were not statistically significant. No apparent differences were noted between the two groups concerning the percentage of subjects sexually involved with multiple partners.

Sexually transmitted diseases were found to be one of the most outstanding characteristics of African-Americans with HIV/AIDS. A history of gonorrhea was reported by 38 percent of the subjects with HIV/AIDS compared to 8 percent of the subjects in the NO-HIV/AIDS group. A history of syphilis was 18 times more likely for subjects with HIV/AIDS, while herpes was 9 times more likely to be part of the health history of individuals with HIV/AIDS. Finally, the percentage of subjects in the YES-HIV/AIDS group with genital warts (38 percent) was significantly higher than for those subjects without HIV/AIDS (45 percent). In other words, individuals with HIV/AIDS were almost 8 times more likely to have a history of genital warts compared to subjects without HIV/AIDS.

In general, the overall pattern of the findings are consistent with what was expected with the exception of two major results. The first was the substantial knowledge deficit concerning key factors associated with the transmission of the AIDS virus among individuals with HIV/AIDS. The second was the absence of a significant difference in the number of individuals sexually involved with multiple partners for subjects with and without HIV/AIDS. While several explanations probably exist for these findings, it is difficult to determine whether they are a reaction to being exposed to HIV/AIDS or whether they were present prior to exposure to the AIDS virus. This is particularly true for the results concerning multiple sex partners because previous research indicates that changes in the number of sexual partners is one of the effects often noted among individuals diagnosed with the AIDS virus. On the other hand, the results con-

cerning the AIDS knowledge deficits are more likely to have contributed to the transmission of the AIDS virus rather than being a reaction
to the diagnosis.

EPILOGUE

Thoughts about the AIDS Crisis among African-Americans

The major purpose of this book has been to examine the interrelationships between knowledge about the transmission of HIV/AIDS, condom use, perceived susceptibility of being exposed to the AIDS virus, drug use, sexually transmitted diseases, and risky sexual behaviors among a well-educated sample of African-American college students. The decision to focus solely on the information obtained from the African-American students was guided by several facts: (1) much of the information we have about the sexual behaviors and attitudes of African-Americans has been gathered from studies of college students and young adults. Therefore, it is possible to determine if the data for this book are consistent with information derived from other studies, and (2) college student populations are much easier to recruit for research studies than other populations of African-Americans. The major disadvantage with this approach is that the information collected and the conclusions reached may not be generalizable or relevant for other population groups. Nevertheless, the use of college students made it possible to conveniently collect information, in a relatively short period of time, from a large sample of African-American males who are routinely difficult to involve in research projects.

There is no doubt that most of what has been written about the health behaviors of individuals with HIV/AIDS is based on white subjects or derived from studies that used African-American subjects as a "control" group to compare to whites. In general, there is nothing wrong with this approach except that it does not permit investigators to understand the variability of risky sexual behaviors within the African-American groups being studied. It is as if the data about

African-Americans are treated as if there are no variations between or within members of the African-American groups. Be this as it may, most investigations of sexual behaviors and attitudes of African-Americans have produced very little useful information and have led to limited generalizations about the specific health behaviors of African-Americans. As a result of these practices, there is not much of an empirical foundation to draw from to develop prevention and treatment programs specifically tailored for African-Americans. Consequently, one of the end results has been the development of insensitive and ineffective HIV/AIDS prevention efforts that are based on information derived from whites, gays, and bisexual males. It is as if the acknowledgment of the cultural differences of minority groups has been treated as a barrier to AIDS education rather than as an issue that is central to the formulation of effective prevention and treatment programs. Recognition of the diversity within ethnic minority groups is very much needed to develop successful educational programs. In the past, the AIDS educational messages have not been sensitive to ethnic diversity, although a disproportionate number of AIDS victims are African-American and Hispanic. As a consequence, the paucity of HIV-related education among African-Americans and other ethnic minority groups during the early stages of the AIDS epidemic continues to have devastating consequences.

The information that you have been reading is based on data gathered from a young adult sample of African-Americans. The findings, no matter how distressful and unnerving, are factual and should be the cause for much concern about the extent of the HIV/AIDS epidemic among African-American young adults. As I see things, African-Americans are undoubtedly at extreme risk for being exposed to HIV/AIDS, and being well-educated does not make you immune to this disease. Of greatest concern is the fact that certain risk factors such as having a history of sexually transmitted diseases and having multiple sex partners are more prevalent among young African-American adults. The potential problems associated with these facts lead one to assume that there is a significant interrelationship between having HIV/AIDS, having a history of sexually transmitted diseases, and having multiple sex partners.

To a great extent, the findings presented in this book strongly indicate that African-Americans with HIV/AIDS are more likely to have a history of sexually transmitted diseases, including those that have been found to be associated with the transmission of the AIDS virus. Even though these results are very similar to those obtained from white samples and other African-American populations, it is now apparent that there was a sexually transmitted disease epidemic among African-Americans long before HIV/AIDS came on the scene.

For example, the prevalence of syphilis is approximately 45 times higher among African-Americans than whites. Similarly, gonorrhea among African-Americans is nearly 34 times the rate for whites. Please note that these figures do not represent new trends, and that the substantially higher rates among African-Americans have been evident for the past 10 to 20 years. These diseases are troubling enough, but the genital ulcers associated with them also increases the risk of exposure to the AIDS virus. Given these observations it is intriguing that very little attention was, or is currently, directed toward the prevention of these STDs among African-Americans. Even so, the fact that because most of the AIDS patients are members of groups which elicit very negative and intolerant public attitudes (e.g., homosexual or bisexual males and IV-drug users), there has been a limited responsiveness to the AIDS health crisis among leaders and members of the African-American community.

In the mind of the public, the AIDS problem is undoubtedly linked to sexual behaviors and possibly perceived to be a result of promiscuity, nonmonogamous sexual activity, and a well-deserved problem that should affect gay and homosexual people. To a certain extent, efforts to combat AIDS in the African-American communities have also been hindered by the fact that we know very little, beyond stereotypes and myths, about the sexuality of African-Americans. It is my belief that these perceptions have provided much of the confusion about what we should do about HIV/AIDS, or for that matter any of the health problems that are at epidemic levels in the African-American communities throughout the United States. It has also been the case that several of the important sources of leadership in the African-American communities have utilized the AIDS epidemic to develop and promote extremely conservative religious and moral agendas and punitive responses toward persons who are already considered to be unfit members of the community. For example, during the first wave of the AIDS epidemic there were several stories within the African-American communities across the United States about ministers who were preaching to their congregations about how AIDS is "God's punishment for homosexual people who sin." While there is no way to determine the extent of this attitude among African-American ministers and preachers, approximately one-fourth of the sample (28 percent) of African-American college students were in agreement with this belief.

There is a long history in the United States of African-Americans and other minority groups being devalued and of having their behavior labeled deviant. In the case of AIDS, the victims are further socially ostracized. A prime example is the fact that Haitians were at one time considered a risk group. Because of this, many Haitians lost their jobs and experienced extreme levels of racial discrimination, not because they had AIDS, but because they were Haitians and therefore linked to AIDS (Moore and LeBaron, 1986).

So, it appears that efforts to combat HIV/AIDS have been hindered by (1) our lack of knowledge about the sexuality of African-Americans, (2) research that has not seriously examined the variability of behavior and attitudes within African-American groups, (3) community and religious leaders who view the AIDS problems as punishment from God, (4) our intolerance of gays and bisexuals within the African-American community, and (5) the lack of attention directed at the prevention of sexually transmitted diseases prior to the HIV/AIDS epidemic. If one accepts these observations, then what are we to do in order to develop effective and culturally sensitive AIDS-prevention messages that will reach African-Americans who are not monogamous, are not abstinent, and who do not use IV-drugs.

One solution is to make sure that African-Americans have an adequate understanding of the factors associated with the transmission of HIV/AIDS. Overall, the pattern of the results indicates that African-Americans are very knowledgeable about AIDS, but there appears to be a gap between knowledge and risky sexual behaviors. The pattern of the findings presented throughout this book suggests that the development of culturally sensitive AIDS-prevention programs for African-American college age adults may be facilitated by considering some of the insights gained from the study. For example, the data suggest the gap between knowledge and risky sexual behavior is likely to be filled with different attitudes and beliefs for males versus females, or individuals with multiple versus non-multiple sexual partners, or individuals with or without a history of STDs, or individuals with or without HIV/AIDS.

Information uncovered by this investigation revealed that males are less knowledgeable about several factors involved in the transmission of AIDS than females. On the other hand, individuals with multiple partners were more likely to believe that AIDS is caused by bacteria or the same virus that causes VD. Knowledge about the factors associated with the transmission of HIV/AIDS was essentially identical for subjects who practiced unprotected anal intercourse and those subjects who did not. Individuals with HIV/AIDS correctly answered only 55 percent of the questions concerning the transmission of AIDS while those not exposed correctly answered 85 percent of the AIDS knowledge questions. These data suggest that educational information and self-assessment instruments may need to be created for and targeted at specific African-American groups rather than rely on a wide-scale mass media campaign to reach all individuals. One way to accomplish this aim may be to create materials that enable African-Americans to actively question and evaluate their own risk.

Perhaps one of the problems that has to be overcome in order to implement such a plan is to identify the explicitness needed in the HIV/AIDS prevention messages for African-Americans who are not monogamous and engaging in risky sexual behaviors (e.g., anal intercourse). I could go on and on about the possible means of how to minimize the gap between knowledge and risky behaviors, but the one way that is likely to result in a more favorable outcome is to simply ask the people involved to provide solutions. Seldom have we taken this position around a major public health problem, but what can we lose by asking African-Americans to generate solutions to problems that are the focus of so much human suffering. I would argue that one of the barriers to effective HIV/AIDS education programs in African-American communities is the fact that the people and organizations have not been encouraged to believe that HIV/AIDS prevention would be more effective when planned, executed, and propagated by members of their own community. In other words, African-American community members are not involved in the empowerment process which stresses both individual determination over one's own life and strong democratic participation in the life of one's community. The notion of empowerment presupposes that African-American community members have the competency to intervene on their own behalf but lack the necessary resources.

It is my belief that HIV/AIDS prevention and intervention efforts will be more effective if and when they use community empowerment as an adjunct to the development and implementation of HIV/AIDS education for African-Americans. I would also argue that once we incorporate principles of empowerment into our strategies for dealing with HIV/AIDS, or the other major health problems present in the African-Americans communities, we will soon discover that the traditional health settings are inappropriate for educating African-Americans who do not routinely use health care facilities. Instead, the most appropriate intervention sites may be the schools, churches, community recreation centers, neighborhood basketball courts, workplaces, fraternities/sororities, and boys and girls clubs such as the Scouts.

Negative attitudes about condoms were more prevalent among males, individuals with multiple partners, and other groups engaging in risky sexual behaviors (e.g., unprotected anal intercourse). What is puzzling is that condoms are an effective means of preventing the spread of STDs, but they tend not to be used by individuals who are more likely to be exposed to STDs (e.g., persons with multiple sex partners, individuals who practice anal intercourse, etc.). Part of the reason for this may be that we have not been effective in teaching these groups to use condoms in a more erotic and fun way. It is evident that large companies can create advertisements that are effective in persuading African-Americans to smoke certain brands of cigarettes and consume certain brands of alcohol. The puzzling issue is why can't as much effort be directed at the use of condoms as is the marketing of cigarettes and alcohol?

Angry reactions about the negotiations of condom use were stronger for males and individuals with multiple partners. The communication problems of African-American males and females are not well outlined, but they may be related to unsafe sexual behaviors such as not using condoms or not acquiring adequate information about the sexual history of a potential partner. In general, males reported a greater intensity of anger when condoms interfered with foreplay and sexual pleasures, while females became angry because their partner insisted on not wearing a condom. The intensity of anger was also greater among males when they thought they would be rejected by their partner(s) if they asked questions about previous sexual contacts. My suggestions to overcome these difficulties involve encouraging African-American adolescents and young adults to learn more about how to communicate effectively and assertively without being destructive.

To cope effectively with angry feelings and reactions, African-Americans must consider a few facts about anger. First, anger is a healthy emotion and a message (a signal) that something is wrong in a relationship and that there is a problem that needs to be addressed. Second, anger is closely related to conflict and having conflict does not necessarily mean that one is incompatible with a partner. In contrast, no two people are alike and there are likely to be differences in personal opinions, values, and the ways of doing things that result in conflict. However, the critical element is not the conflict, but how the conflict is handled. Finally, angry feelings and reactions can either be talked out or acted out. Much of the problem with anger is that when it is acted out, aggression and violent behaviors are likely to be the driving force behind the responses. Also, the probability increases that issues will not be addressed in a constructive way because the intent is to overpower and hurt rather than to understand and find a workable solution to a problem. Perhaps pointing out these issues in commercials and magazines read by African-Americans would help to convey the full extent that AIDS is affecting this community.

As indicated earlier, marketing techniques have been used successfully within the African-American communities to motivate the group to purchase particular brands of cigarettes, liquor, and basket-ball shoes. However, no attention, as of yet, has been given to the development of those thirty-second commercials that motivate African-Americans to develop powerful health-promoting associations between our emotions (i.e., being angry about a partner who refuses to use a condom) and the behavior of others. Because television and other media significantly impact the behavior of adults and children, there is a strong need for our society to impose stricter controls over the content of materials disseminated through these channels. For example, some rather strong and positive associations have been developed between having multiple sex partners, drugs, and making "easy money" in several movies directed at African-Americans. In contrast, what is needed are examples showing African-Americans who are successful in avoiding risk situations by adopting alternatives to high-risk behaviors.

The information presented throughout this book also indicates that there is a large gap in people's perceptions of their risk for AIDS, their involvement in risky sexual behaviors, as well as their knowledge about factors related to the transmission of AIDS. A major reason for these difficulties may be that public health professionals have not been effective in getting people to critically evaluate their own risk for HIV and AIDS. However, there are two sides to this issue. One involves the problems associated with changing the unhealthy lifestyle of African-Americans, while the other involves inequities in the health care delivery system and the cold and indifferent manner in which African-Americans are received. It could be that we have not developed prevention and intervention strategies that fully consider the unique problems associated with working with patients who are poor, not well-educated, and without insurance. We need to create materials that actively involve individuals in the assessment and evaluation of their own risk. Instead of accepting the fact that HIV/AIDS is spreading rapidly among African-Americans, there is a need for each of us to teach ourselves and our children about responsible sexual behavior and to become completely honest with ourselves about whether or not we actually practice safe and reponsible sex. The truth may be that for many African-Americans, there may be some serious misconceptions about responsible sex.

References

Adams, R. (1987). The role of prostitution in AIDS and other STDs. *Medical Aspects of Human Sexuality, 21,* 27–33.

AIDS among women to double by 2000. (1991, March–April). *Public Health Reports, 106* (2), 216.

Alter, M. J., Francis, D., and the CDC Sentinel Country Study Group Centers for Disease Control. (1987, June). *Evidence of reduced AIDS associated risk behavior in homosexual/bisexual men but not in heterosexuals or IV drug users in 4 widely dispersed U.S. counties.* Paper presented to the Third International Conference on AIDS, Washington, DC.

Amaro, H. *HIV Prevention with Ethnic Minority Women: Lessons from a project targeted at pregnant women.* Presented at the 98th Annual American Psychological Association Convention, Boston, MA, August 12, 1990.

Anderson, R. E., and Levy, J. A. (1985). Prevalence of antibodies to AIDS-associated retrovirus in single men in San Francisco. *Lancet, 1,* 217.

Antibody to human immunodeficiency virus in female prostitutes. (1987). *Morbidity and Mortality Weekly Report, 36,* 157–161.

Aral, S. O., Cates, W., Jr., and Jenkins, W. C. (1985). Genital herpes: Does knowledge lead to action? *American Journal of Public Health, 75,* 69–71.

Bachman, J. G., Wallace, J. M., O'Malley, P. M., Johnston, L. D., Kurth, C. L., and Neighbors, H. W. (1991). Racial/ethnic differences in smoking, drinking, and illicit drug use among American high school seniors 1976–1989. *American Journal of Public Health, 81,* 372–377.

Baffi, C. R., Schroeder, K. K., Redican, K. J., and McCluskey, L. (1989). Factors influencing selected heterosexual college students' condom use. *Journal of American College Health, 38,* 137–141.

Bakerman, R., McCray, E., Lumb, J. R., Jackson, R. E., and Whitley, P. N. (1987). The incidence of AIDS among Blacks and Hispanics. *Journal of the National Medical Association, 79,* 921–928.

Baldwin, J. D., and Baldwin, J. I. (1988a). AIDS information and sexual behavior on a university campus. *Field Reports, 14,* 24–28.

――. (1988b). Factors affecting AIDS-related sexual risk-taking behavior among college students. *Journal of Sex Research, 25,* 181–196.

Bayer, H., Bienzle, U., Schneider, J., and Hunsmann, G. (1984). HTLV-III antibody frequency and severity of lymphadenopathy. *Lancet, 2,* 1347.

Becker, T. M., Stone, K. M., and Cates, W., Jr. (1986). Epidemiology of genital herpes infections in the United States: The current situation. *Journal of Reproductive Medicine, 31,* 359–366.

Bell, D., Feraios, A., and Bryan, T. (1990). Adolescent males' knowledge and attitudes about AIDS in the context of their social world. *Journal of Applied Social Psychology, 20,* 424–448.

Berg, A. O. (1990). The primary care physician and sexually transmitted disease control. In Holmes, K. K. (Ed.), *Sexually Transmitted Diseases* (2nd ed.), pp. 1095–1098. New York: McGraw-Hill.

Biglan, A., Metzler, C. W., Wirt, R., Ary, D., Noell, J., Ochs, L., French, C., and Hood, D. (1990). Social and behavioral factors associated with high-risk sexual behavior among adolescents. *Journal of Behavioral Medicine, 13,* 245–261.

Blattner, W. A., Biggar, R. J., Weiss, S. H., Melbye, M., and Goedert, J. J. (1985). Epidemiology of human T-lymphotrophic virus type III and the risk of the acquired immunodeficiency syndrome. *Annals of Internal Medicine, 103,* 665–670.

Bolling, D. R., Jr. (1977). Prevalence, goals and complications of heterosexual anal intercourse in a gynecologic population. *Journal of Reproductive Medicine, 19* (3), 120–124.

Bolling, D. R., Jr., and Voeller, B. (1987). AIDS and heterosexual anal intercourse. *Journal of the American Medical Association, 258,* 474.

Boyer, C., and Schafer, R. (1990, August). *Symposium on adolescent attitudes toward condom use.* Presented at the scientific meetings of the American Psychological Association, Boston.

Broman, C. L., and Johnson, E. H. (1988). Anger expression and life stress among blacks: Their role in physical health. *Journal of the National Medical Association, 80* (12), 1329–1334.

Brooks, G. F., Darrow, W. W., and Day, J. A. (1978, February). Repeated gonorrhea: an analysis of importance and risk factors. *Journal of Infectious Diseases, 137* (2), 161–169.

Brooner, R. K., Bigelow, G. E., Strain, E., and Schmidt, C. W. (1990). Intravenous drug abusers with antisocial personality disorder: Increased HIV risk behavior. *Drug and Alcohol Dependence, 26,* 39–44.

Brown, L. K., and Fritz, G. K. (1988). AIDS education in the schools. *Clinical Pediatrics, 27,* 311–316.

Brown, L. S. (1984). Development of a scale to measure attitudes toward the condom as a measure of birth control. *Journal of Sex Research, 20,* 255–263.

Brown, L. S., Jr., and Primm, B. J. (1988). Sexual contacts of intravenous drug abusers: Implications for the next spread of the AIDS epidemic. *Journal of the National Medical Association, 80,* 651–656.

Brunham, R. C., Paavonen, J., Stevens, C. E., Kiviat, N., Kuo, C. C., Critchlow, C. W., and Holmes, K. K. (1984). Mucopurulent cervicitis – the ignored counterpart in women of urethritis in men. *New England Journal of Medicine, 311,* 1–6.

Buffum, J. (1988). Substance abuse and high-risk sexual behavior: Drugs and sex—the dark side. *Journal of Psychoactive Drugs, 20,* 165–168.

Bump, R. C., Sachls, L. A., and Buesching, W. J. T. (1986). Sexually transmittable infectious agents in sexually active and virginal asymptomatic adolescent girls. *Pediatrics, 77,* 488–494.

Burger, J. M., and Burns, L. (1988). The illusion of vulnerability and the use of effective contraception. *Personality and Social Psychology Bulletin, 14,* 264–270.

Burnette, M. M., Redmon, W. K., and Poling, A. (1990). Knowledge, attitudes and behavior of college undergraduates regarding acquired immune deficiency syndrome. *College Student Journal, 24,* 27–38.

Calabrese, L. H., and Gopalakrishna, K. V. (1986). Transmission of HTLV-III infection from man to woman to man. *New England Journal of Medicine, 314,* 987.

Carlson, J. R., Bryant, M. L., Hinrichs, S. H., Yamamoto, J. K., Levy, N. B., Yee, J., Higgins, J., Levine, A. M., Holland, P., Gardner, M. B., and Pedersen, N. C. (1985). AIDS serology testing in low-and-high-risk groups. *Journal of the American Medical Association, 253,* 3405–3408.

Catania, J. A., Coates, T. J., Kegeles, S. M., Ekstrand, M., Guydish, J., and Bye, L. (1989). Implications of the AIDS risk reduction model for the homosexual community: The importance of perceived sexual enjoyment and help-seeking behaviors. In V. Mays, G. Albee, J. Jones, and J. Schneider (Eds.), *Psychological approaches to the prevention of AIDS* (pp. 242–261). Beverly Hills: Sage.

Catania, J. A., Coates, T. J., Stall, R., Bye, L., Capell, F., Henne, J., McKusick, L., Morin, S., Turner, H., and Pollack, L. (1991). Changes in condom use among homosexual men in San Francisco. *Health Psychology, 10,* 190–199.

Catania, J. A., Dolcini, M. M., Coates, T. J., Kegeles, S. M., Greenblatt, R. M., Puckett, S., Corman, M., and Miller, J. (1989). Predictors of condom use and multiple partnered sex among sexually active adolescent women: Implications for AIDS-related health interventions. *Journal of Sex Research, 26,* 514–524.

Catania, J. A., Kegeles, S. M., and Coates, T. J. (1990). Toward an understanding of risk behaviors: An AIDS risk reduction model (ARRM). *Health Education Quarterly, 17,* 381–399.

Cates, W., Jr. (1988). The other STDs: Do they really matter? *Journal of the American Medical Association, 259* (24), 3606–3608.

Cates, W., Jr., and Toomey, K. E. (1990). Sexually transmitted diseases—Overview of the situation. *Sexually Transmitted Diseases, 17* (19), 1–27.

Centers for Disease Control. (1987, September). *HIV/AIDS Surveillance Report,* 1–16.

———. (1991, September). *HIV/AIDS Surveillance Report,* 1–18.

———. (1981a). Pneumocystis pneumonia—Los Angeles. *Morbidity and Mortality Weekly Report, 30,* 250–252.

———. (1981b). Kaposi's sarcoma and pneumonia among homosexual men—

New York City and California. *Morbidity and Mortality Weekly Report,* *30,* 305–308.

——. (1983). Update: Acquired immunodeficiency syndrome (AIDS)—United States. *Morbidity and Mortality Weekly Report, 32,* 465–467.

——. (1987). Increases in primary and secondary syphilis—United States. *Morbidity and Mortality Weekly Report, 36,* 393–397.

——. (1988a). The extent of AIDS and indicators of adolescent risk. *Morbidity and Mortality Weekly Report, 37,* 10–14.

——. (1988b). Number of sex partners and potential risk of sexual exposure to HIV. *Morbidity and Mortality Weekly Report, 37,* 565–568.

——. (1989a). AIDS and human immunodeficiency virus infection in the United States: 1988 update. *Morbidity and Mortality Weekly Report, 38,* 1–31.

——. (1989b). AIDS and human immunodeficiency virus infection in the United States: 1988 update. *Morbidity and Mortality Weekly Report, 38* (Suppl. 4), 1–38.

——. (1990a). AIDS in women—United States. *Morbidity and Mortality Weekly Report, 39* (47), 845–846.

——. (1990b). Heterosexual behaviors and factors that influence condom use among patients attending a sexually transmitted disease clinic—San Francisco. *Morbidity and Mortality Weekly Report, 39,* 685–689.

——. (1990c). HIV prevalence estimates and AIDS case projections for the United States: Report based on a workshop. *Morbidity and Mortality Weekly Report, 39,* 1–31.

——. (1991a). *HIV/AIDS Surveillance Report,* 5–18.

——. (1991b). Mortality attributable to HIV infection/AIDS—United States, 1981–1990. *Morbidity and Mortality Weekly Report, 40,* 41–44.

——. (1991c). Update: Years of potential life lost before age 65—United States, 1988 and 1989. *Morbidity and Mortality Weekly Report, 40,* 60–62.

Chu, S. Y., Buehler, J. W., and Berkelman, R. C. (1990). Impact of the human immunodeficiency virus epidemic on mortality in women of reproductive age, United States. *Journal of the American Medical Association, 264,* 225–229.

Clark, S. D., Zabin, L. S., and Hardy, J. B. (1984). Sex, contraception and parenthood: experience and attitudes among urban Black young men. *Family Planning Perspectives, 16,* 77–82.

Clumeck, N., Sonnet, J., Taelman, H., Mascart-Lemone, F., DeBruyere, M., Van de Perre, P., Dashnoy, J., Marcelis, L., Lamy, M., Jonas, C., Eycksmans, L., Noel, H., Vanhaverbeek, M., and Butzler, J. P. (1984). Acquired immunodeficiency syndrome in African patients. *New England Journal of Medicine, 310,* 492–497.

Clumeck, N., Van de Perre, P., Carael, M., Rouvroy, D., and Nzaramba, D. (1985). Heterosexual promiscuity in African patients with AIDS. *New England Journal of Medicine, 313,* 182.

Coates, T. J. (1990). Strategies for modifying sexual behavior for primary and secondary prevention of HIV disease. *Journal of Consulting and Clinical Psychology, 58,* 57–69.

Coates, T. J., Morin, S. F., and McKusick, L. (1987, June). *Consequences of AIDS antibody testing among gay men: The AIDS behavioral research project.* Paper presented to the Third International Conference on AIDS, Washington, DC.

Coates, T. J., Stall, R., Catania, J., and Kegeles, S. M. (1988). Behavioral factors in the spread of HIV infection. *AIDS,* vol. 2 (Suppl. 1): S239–S246.

Cottler, L. B., Helzer, J. E, and Tipp, J. E. (1990). Lifetime patterns of substance abuse among general population subjects engaging in high risk sexual behaviors: Implications for HIV risk. *American Journal of Drug and Alcohol Abuse, 16,* 207–222.

Council on Scientific Affairs status report on the acquired immunodeficiency syndrome human T-cell lymphotropic virus type III testing. (1985). *Journal of the American Medical Association, 254,* 1342–1345.

Curran, J. W. (1985). The epidemiology and prevention of acquired immunodeficiency syndrome. *Annals of Internal Medicine, 103,* 657–662.

Curran, J. W., Morgan, W. M., Starcher, E. T., Hardy, A. M., and Jaffe, H. W. (1985). Epidemiological trends of AIDS in the United States. *Cancer Research, 45,* 4602s–4604s.

Darrow, W. W. (1976). Venereal infections in three ethnic groups in Sacramento. *American Journal of Public Health, 66,* 446–450.

———. (1986). Sexual behavior in America: Implications for the control of sexually transmitted diseases. In Feldman (Ed.), *Sexually Transmitted Diseases* (pp. 261–290). New York: Churchill Livingstone.

———. (1987, February). *Condom Use and Use-Effectiveness in High Risk Populations.* Paper presented at the Conference on Condoms in the Prevention of Sexually Transmitted Diseases, Centers for Disease Control, Atlanta.

———. (1988, August). *The Potential Spread of HIV Infection in Female Prostitutes.* Paper presented at the annual meeting of the American Psychological Association, New York.

Darrow, W. W., Jaffe, H., and Curran, J. (1983). Passive anal intercourse as a risk factor for AIDS in homosexual men. *Lancet, 2,* 160.

Dax, E. M., Adler, W. H., Dorsey, B. A., and Jaffe, J. H. (1987, June). *Amyl-nitrite inhalation alters immune function in normal volunteers.* Paper presented to the Third International Conference on AIDS, Washington, DC.

Des Jarlis, D. C., Wish, E., Friedman, S. R., Stoneburner, R., Yancovitz, S. R., Mildvan, D., el-Sadr, W., Brady, E., and Cuadrado, M. (1987). Intravenous drug users and the heterosexual transmission of the acquired immunodeficiency syndrome. *New York State Journal of Medicine, 87,* 283–286.

Detels, R., English, P., Visscher, B., Jacobson, L., Kingsley, L., Chimel, J., Dudley, J., Eldered, L., and Ginzburg, H. (1989). Seroconversion, sexual activity, and condom use and 2,915 HIV seronegative men followed for up to 2 years. *Journal of Acquired Immune Deficiency Syndrome, 2,* 77–83.

Detels, R., Visscher, B., Kingsley, L., and Chimel, J. (1987, June). *No HIV seroconversion among men refraining from anal-genital intercourse.* Paper presented to the Third International Conference on AIDS, Washington, DC.

DiClemente, R. J. (1989). Prevention of human immunodeficiency virus infection among adolescents: The interplay of health education and public policy in the development and implementation of school-based AIDS education programs. *AIDS Education and Prevention, 1,* 70–78.

DiClemente, R. J., Boyer, C. B., and Morales, E. S. (1988). Minorities and AIDS: Knowledge, attitudes, and misconceptions among Black and Latino adolescents. *American Journal of Public Health, 78,* 55–57.

DiClemente, R. J., Zorn, J., and Temoshok, L. (1987). The association of gender, ethnicity, and length of residence in the bay area to adolescents' knowledge and attitudes about acquired immune deficiency syndrome. *Journal of Applied Social Psychology, 17,* 216–230.

Division of Sexually Transmitted Diseases. (1988). *Sexually Transmitted Disease Statistics, 1987, 136.* Atlanta: Centers for Disease Control.

Edwards, A. (1991, February). You, me, and he. *Essence,* 59–110.

Egeland, J. A. (1978). Ethnic value orientation analysis: A research component of the Miami health ecology project. Miami: University of Miami, Department of Psychiatry.

Elkind, D. (1978). Understanding the young adolescent. *Adolescence, 13,* 127–134.

Feldblum, P., and Fortney, J. (1988). Condoms, spermicides and the transmission of HIV: A review of the literature. *American Journal of Public Health, 78,* 52–54.

Feldman, H. W., and Biernacki, P. (1988). The ethnography of needle sharing among intravenous drug users and implications for public policies and intervention strategies. In R. Battjes and R. Pickens, (Eds.), *The needle sharing among intravenous drug abusers: National and international perspectives.* NIDA Research Monograph #80. Rockville, MD: U.S. Department of Health and Human Services.

Fichtner, R. R., Aral, S. O., Blount, J. H., Zaidi, A. A., Reynolds, G. H., and Darrow, W. W. (1983). Syphilis in the United States: 1967–1979. *Sexually Transmitted Diseases, 10,* 77–80.

Fischl, M. A., Dickinson, G. M., Scott, G. B., Klimas, N., Fletcher, M. A., and Parks, W. (1987). Evaluation of heterosexual partners, children, and household contacts of adults with AIDS. *Journal of the American Medical Association, 257,* 640–644.

Fisher, J. (1988). Possible effects of reference group-based social influence on AIDS-risk behavior and AIDS prevention. *American Psychologist, 43,* 907–913.

Flaskerud, J. D., and Nyamathi, A. M. (1989, December). Black and Latino women: AIDS related knowledge, attitudes, and practices. *Research in Nursing and Health, 16* (6), 339–366.

Flynn, N. M., Jain, S., Harper, S., Bailey, B., Anderson, R., and Acuna, G. (1987, June). *Sharing of paraphernalia in intravenous drug users (IVDU): Knowledge of AIDS is incomplete and doesn't affect behavior.* Paper presented to the Third International Conference on AIDS, Washington, DC.

Fox, R., Ostrow, D., Valdiserri, R., Van Radden, M., Visscher, B., and Polk, B. F. (1987, June). *Changes in sexual activities among participants in the multicenter AIDS cohort study.* Paper presented to the Third International Conference on AIDS, Washington, DC.

Francis, D. P., and Petriccian, J. C. (1985). The prospects for and pathways toward a vaccine for AIDS. *New England Journal of Medicine, 313,* 1586–1590.

Fullilove, M. T. (1989). Anxiety and stigmatizing aspects of HIV infection. *Journal of Clinical Psychiatry, 50,* 5–8.

Fullilove, M. T., and Fullilove, R. E. (1989). Intersecting epidemics: Black teen crack use and sexually transmitted disease. *Journal of the American Medical Women's Association 44* (5), 145–153.

Fullilove, M. T., Fullilove, R. E., Haynes, K., and Gross, S. (1990). Black women and AIDS: A view toward understanding the gender rules. *Journal of Sex Research, 27,* 47–64.

Fullilove, R. E., Fullilove, M. T., Bowser, B., and Gross, S. (1990a). Crack users: The new AIDS risk group? *Cancer Detection and Prevention, 14,* 363–368.

——. (1990b). Risk of sexually transmitted diseases among Black adolescent crack users in Oakland and San Francisco, California. *Sexually Transmitted Diseases, 263,* 851–855.

Fumento, M. (1990). *The Myth of Heterosexual AIDS.* New York: Basic Books.

Gayle, J. A., Selik, R. M., and Chu, S. Y. (1990). Surveillance for AIDS and HIV infection among Black and Hispanic children and women of childbearing age, 1981–1989. Center for Infectious Diseases. *Morbidity and Mortality Weekly Report, 39,* (Suppl. 3), 1–8.

Gibson, J. J., Hornung, C. A., Alexander, G. R., Lee, F. K., Potts, W. A., and Nahmias, A. J. (1988). A cross-sectional study of herpes simplex virus types 1 and 2 in college students: Occurrence and determinants of infection. *The Journal of Infectious Diseases, 162,* 306–312.

Goedert, J. J. (1985). Recreational drugs: Relationship to AIDS. *Annals of the New York Academy of Sciences, 437,* 192–199.

Goedert, J. J., Sarngadharan, M. G., Biggar, R. J., Weiss, S. H., Winn, D. M., Grossman, R. J., Greene, M. H., Bodner, A. J., Mann, D. L., Strong, D. M., Gallo, R. C., and Blattner, W. A. (1984). Determinants of retrovirus (HTLV-III) antibody and immunodeficiency conditions in homosexual men. *Lancet, 2,* 711–716.

Goedert, J. J., Sarngadharan, M. G., Eyster, M. E., Weiss, S. H., Bodner, A. J., Gallo, R. C., and Blattner, W. A. (1985). Antibodies reactive with human T-cell leukemia viruses in the serum of hemophiliacs receiving factor 3 concentration. *Blood, 65,* 492–495.

Goldsmith, M. F. (1987). Sex in the age of AIDS calls for common sense and "condom sense." *Journal of the American Medical Association, 257,* 2261–2263, 2266.

——. (1988). Sex tied to drugs equals STD spread. *Journal of the American Medical Association, 260,* 2009.

Goodwin, M. P., and Roscoe, B. (1988). AIDS: Students' knowledge and attitudes at a midwestern university. *Journal of American College Health, 36,* 214–222.

Groopman, J. E. (1985). Clinical spectrum of HTLV-III in humans. *Cancer Research, 45,* 4649s–4651s.

Grubbs, G. S. (1986). Human papillomavirus and cervical neoplasis: Epidemiological considerations. *International Journal of Epidemiology, 15,* 1–16.

Guinan, M. E., and Hardy, A. (1987). Epidemiology of AIDS in women in the United States: 1981 through 1986. *Journal of the American Medical Association, 257,* 2039–2042.

Guinan, M. E., Wolinsky, S. M., and Reichman, R. C. (1985). Epidemiology of genital herpes simplex virus infection. *Epidemiology Review, 7,* 127–146.

Hammonds, E. (1987). Race, Sex, AIDS: The construction of "other." *Radical America, 20,* 28–36.

Handsfield, H. H. (1981). Sexually transmitted diseases in homosexual men. *American Journal of Public Health, 71* (9), 989–990.

Handsfield, H. H. (1985). Decreasing incidence of gonorrhea in homosexually active men—minimal effect on AIDS. *Western Journal of Medicine, 143,* 469–474. Atlanta, GA: Centers for Disease Control.

Hiebert, Y., Bernard, J., De Man, A. F., and Farrar, D. (1988). Factors related to the use of condoms among French-Canadian university students. *The Journal of Social Psychology, 129,* 707–709.

Hernandez, J. T., and Smith, F. J. (1990). Inconsistencies and misperceptions putting college students at risk of HIV infection. *Journal of Adolescent Health Care, 11,* 295–297.

Hessol, N. A., Rutherford, G. W., O'Malley, P. M., Doll, L. S., Darrow, W. W., and Jaffe, H. W. (1987, June). *The natural history of human immunodeficiency virus infection in a cohort of homosexual and bisexual men: A 7-year prospectus study.* Paper presented to the Third International Conference on AIDS, Washington, DC.

Hill, I. (1987). *The Bisexual Spouse.* McLean, VA: Barlina Books.

Hingson, R., Strunin, L., Craven, L., Mangione, T., Berlin, B., Amaro, H., and Lamb, G. (1989). A statewide survey of AIDS knowledge and behavior change among Massachusetts adults. *Preventive Medicine, 18,* 806–816.

Ho, D. D., Byington, R. E., Schooley, R. T., Flynn, T., Rota, T. R., and Hirsh, M. S. (1985). Infrequency of isolation of HTLV-III virus from saliva in AIDS. *New England Journal of Medicine, 313,* 1606.

Houck, C. (1984). Why married men will still pay for sex. *Ladies Home Journal, 101,* (3), 60.

Hunt, M. (1974). *Sexual Behavior in the 1970s.* Chigago: Playboy Press.

Ishii-Kuntz, M. (1988). Acquired immune deficiency syndrome and sexual behavior changes in a college student sample. *Sociology and Social Research, 73,* 13–18.

Jackson, J. (1973). Black women in a racist society. In C. V. Willie, B. M. Krammer, and B. S. Brown (Eds.), *Racism and Mental Health.* Pittsburgh: University of Pittsburgh Press.

Jackson, J. (1971, December). But where are the men? *The Black Scholar,* 30–41.

Jaffe, H. W., Biddle, J. W., Johnson, S. R., and Wiesner, P. J. (1981). Infections due to penicillinase-producing Neisseria gonorrhoeae in the U.S. 1976–1980. *Journal of Infectious Disease, 144,* 191–196.

Jaffe, H. W., Darrow, W. W., Echenberg, D. F., O'Malley, P. M., Getchell, J. P., Kalyanaram, V. S., Byers, R. H., Drennan, D. P., Braff, E. H., Curran, J. N., and Francis, D. P. (1985). The acquired immunodeficiency syndrome in a cohort of homosexual men. *Annals of Internal Medicine, 103,* 210–214.

Jaffe, L. R., Seehaus, M., Wagner, C., and Leadbeater, B. J. (1988). Anal intercourse and knowledge of acquired immunodeficiency syndrome among minority-group female adolescents. *The Journal of Pediatrics, 112,* 1005–1007.

Johnson, E. H. (1984). *Anger and Anxiety as Determinants of Blood Pressure in Adolescents: The Tampa Study.* Doctoral Dissertation, Department of Psychology, University of South Florida, Tampa.

——. (1989). Psychiatric Morbidity and Health Problems among Black Americans: A National Survey. *Journal of the National Medical Association, 81* (12), 1217–1223.

——. (1990a). *The Deadly Emotions: The Role of Anger, Hostility and Aggression in Health and Emotional Well-being.* New York: Praeger.

——. (1990b). Interrelationships between psychological factors, overweight, and blood pressure in adolescents. *Journal of Adolescent Health Care, 11,* 310–318.

Johnson, E. H., and Broman, C. L. (1987). Anger expression and health problems among black Americans in a national survey. *Journal of Behavioral Medicine, 10,* 103–116.

Johnson, E. H., Gant, L. M., Hinkle, Y. A., and Gilbert, D. (1992). Black males who always use condoms: Their attitudes, knowledge about AIDS and sexual behaviors. *Journal of the National Medical Association, 84,* 341–352.

Johnson, E. H., Gant, L. M., Hinkle, Y. A., Gilbert, D., Willis, C., and Hoopwood, T. (1992). Do African-American males and females differ in their knowledge about AIDS, attitudes about condoms and sexual behaviors? *Journal of the National Medical Association, 84,* 49–64.

Johnson, E. H., Gant, L. M., Jackson, L., Gilbert, D. A., and Willis, C. (1991, March 20–23). *Multiple sex partners, knowledge about AIDS, and attitudes about using condoms among black males.* Paper presented at the Society of Behavioral Medicine, 12-Annual Scientific Sessions, Washington, DC.

Johnson, E. H., Gant, L. M., Jackson, L., Gilbert, D. A., and Willis, C. A. (1991). *Multiple partners, condom use, and knowledge about AIDS in black males.* (Abstract) Society for Behavioral Medicine, Washington, DC.

Johnson, E. H., and Gilbert, G. (1991). Familial and psychological determinants of smoking in adolescents. *Ethnicity and Disease, 1,* 320–334.

Johnson, R. E., Nahamias, A. J., Magder, L. S., Lee, F. K., Brooks, C. A., and Snowden, C. B. (1989). Distribution of genital herpes (HSV-2) in the United States: A seroepidemiological national survey using a new type-specific antibody assay. *New England Journal of Medicine, 321,* 7–12.

Johnson, E. H., Schork, N., and Spielberger, C. D. (1987). Emotional and familial determinants of elevated blood pressure in black and white adolescent females. *Journal of Psychosomatic Research, 31,* 731–741.

Johnson, E. H., Spielberger, C. D., Worden, T. J., and Jacobs, G. A. (1987). Emotional and familial determinants of elevated blood pressure in black and white adolescent males. *Journal of Psychosomatic Research, 31,* 287–300.

Joseph, J. G., Montgomery, S., Kessler, R. C., Ostrow, D. G., Emmons, C. A., and Phair, J. P. (1987, June). *Two-year longitudinal study of behavioral risk reduction in a cohort of homosexual men.* Paper presented to the Third International Conference on AIDS, Washington, DC.

Judson, F., Miller, K., and Schaffnit, T. (1977). Screening for gonorrhea and syphilis in the gay baths—Denver, Colorado. *American Journal of Public Health, 67,* 740–742.

Judson, F. N. (1983). Fear of AIDS and gonorrhea rates in homosexual men. *Lancet, 2,* 159.

Judson, F. N., Penley, K. A., Robinson, M. E., and Smith, J. K. (1980). Comparative prevalence rates of sexually transmitted diseases in heterosexual and homosexual men. *American Journal of Epidemiology, 112,* 836–843.

Kegeles, S. M., Adler, N. E., and Irwin, C. E. (1988). Sexually active adolescents and condoms: Changes over one year in knowledge, attitudes and use. *American Journal of Public Health, 78,* 460–461.

Kegels, S., Catania, J. A., and Coates, T. J. (1987, June). *Motivations and consequences of AIDS antibody testing among heterosexuals.* Paper presented to the Third International Conference on AIDS, Washington, DC.

Keller, S. E., Bartlett, J. A., Schleifer, S. J., Johnson, R. L., Pinner, E., and Delaney, B. (1991). HIV-relevant sexual behavior among a healthy innercity heterosexual adolescent population in an endemic area of HIV. - *Journal of Adolescent Health, 12,* 44–48.

Kelly, J. A., and St. Lawrence, J. S. (1988). *The AIDS Health Crisis: Psychological and Social Interventions.* New York: Plenum Press.

Kinsey, A. C., and the Institute for Sex Research. (1953). *Sexual Behavior in the Human Female.* Philadelphia: W. B. Saunders.

Kinsey, A. C., Pomeroy, W. B., and Martin, C. E. (1948). *Sexual Behavior in the Human Female.* Philadelphia: W. B. Saunders.

Koop, C. E. (1986). *Surgeon General's Report on Acquired Immune Deficiency Syndrome.* Washington, DC: U.S. Public Health Service.

Koutsky, L. A., Galloway, D. A., and Holmes, K. K. (1988). Epidemiology of genital human pappilloma-virus infection. *Epidemiology Review, 10,* 122–163.

Kovacs, J. A., and Masur, H. (1984). Treatment of opportunistic infections. In P. Ebbesen, R. S. Biggar, and M. Melbyer (Eds.), *AIDS-A basic guide for clinicians* (pp. 84–98). Copenhagen: Munksgaard.

Landrum, S., Beck-Sague, C., and Kraus, S. (1988). Racial trends in syphilis among men with same-sex partners in Atlanta, Georgia. *American Journal of Public Health, 78,* 66–67.

Lang, W., Anderson, R. E., Perkins, H., Gant, R. M., Winkelstein, W., Jr., Royce, R., and Levy, J. A. (1987). The San Francisco Men's Health Study: II Clinical, immunologic, and serologic findings in men at risk for AIDS. *Journal of the American Medical Association, 257* (3), 326–330.

Lange, W. R., Snyder, F. R., Lozovsky, D., Kaistha, V., Kaczaniuk, M. A., and Jaffe, J. H. (1988). Geographic distribution of human immunodeficiency virus markers in parental drug abusers. *American Journal of Public Health, 78,* 443–446.

Lewis, D. K., and Watters, J. K. (1988). HIV seroprevalence and needle sharing among heterosexual intravenous drug users: Ethnic/gender comparisons (letter). *American Journal of Public Health, 78,* 1499.

——. (1989). Human immunodeficiency virus seroprevalence in female intravenous drug users: The puzzle of black women's risk. *Social Science and Medicine, 29,* 1071–1076.

Lloyd, R. (1976). *For Money or Love: Boy Prostitution in America.* New York: Ballantine.

Luria, Z., Friedman, S., and Rose, M. D. (1987). *Human Sexuality.* New York: John D. Wiley and Sons.

MacDonald, N. E., Wells, G. A., Fisher, W. A., Warren, W. K., King, M. A., Doherty, J. A., and Bowie, W. R. (1990). High-risk STD/HIV behavior among college students. *Journal of the American Medical Association, 263,* 3155–3159.

Macher, A. M., and Reichert, C. M (1984). The pathological findings associated with opportunistic infections in AIDS. In P. Ebbesen, R. S. Baggar, and M. Melbye (Eds.), *AIDS-A basic guide for clinicians* (pp. 113–122). Copenhagen: Munksgaard.

Madhubuti, H. R. (1990). Black Men: Obsolete, Single, Dangerous? *African-American Families in Transition: Essays in Discovery, Solution and Hope.* Chicago: Third World Press.

Magura, S., Shapiro, J. L., Grossman, J. I., and Lipton, D. S. (1989). Education/support groups for AIDS prevention with at-risk clients. Social Casework: *The Journal of Contemporary Social Work,* 10–20.

Manning, D. T., Barenberg, N., Gallese, L., and Rice, J. C. (1989). College students' knowledge and health beliefs about AIDS: Implications for education and prevention. *Journal of American College Health, 37,* 254–259.

Marmor, M., Friedman-Kien, A. E., Laubenstein, L., Byrum, R. D., William, D. C., D'Onofrio, S., and Dubin, N. (1982). Risk factors for Karposi's sarcoma in homosexual men. *Lancet, 1,* 1083–1086.

Martin, J. L. (1990). Drug use and unprotected anal intercourse among gay men. *Health Psychology, 9* (4), 450–465.

Mays, V. M., and Cochran, S. D. (1988). Issues in the perception of AIDS risk and risk reduction activities by black and hispanic women. *American Psychologist, 43,* 949–957.

McCusker, L., Stoddard, A. M., Mayer, K. H., Zapka, J., Morrison, C., and Saltzman, S. P. (1988). Effects of HIV antibody test knowledge on subsequent sexual behaviors in a cohort of homosexual men. *American Journal of Public Health, 78,* 462–467.

McKusick, L., Coates, T. J., Wiley, J., Morin, S., and Stall, R. (1987, June). *Prevention of HIV infection among gay and bisexual men: Two longitudinal studies.* Paper presented at the International Conference on AIDS, Washington, DC.

Melbye, M., Biggar, R. J., Ebbesen, P., Sarngadharan, M. G., Weiss, S. H., Gallo, R. C., and Blattner, W. A. (1984). Seroepidemiology of HTLV-III antibody in Danish homosexual active men: Prevalence, transmission, and disease outcome. *British Medical Journal, 289,* 573–575.

Melchert, T., and Burnett, K. F. (1990). Attitudes, knowledge, and sexual behavior of high-risk adolescents: Implications for counseling and sexuality education. *Journal of Counseling and Development, 68,* 293–298.

Mertz, G. J., Coombs, R. W., Asley, R., Jourden, J., Remington, M., Winters,

C., Fahnlander, A., Guinan, M., Ducey, H., and Corey, L. (1988). Transmission of genital herpes in couples with one symptomatic and asymptomatic partner: A prospective study. *Journal of Infectious Diseases, 157,* 1169–1177.

Moore, A., and LeBaron, R. D. (1986). The case for a Haitian origin of the AIDS epidemic. In D. A. Feldman and T. M. Johnson (Eds.), *The Social Dimensions of AIDS.* New York: Praeger.

Moran, J. S., Aral, S. O., Jenkins, W. C., Peterman, T. A., and Alexander, E. R. (1988). The impact of sexually transmitted diseases on minority populations. *Public Health Reports, 104,* 560–565.

Moss, G. B., and Kreiss, J. K. (1990). The interrelationship between human immunodeficiency virus infection and other sexually transmitted diseases. *Medical Clinics of North America, 74,* 1647–1660.

Newell, G. R., Mansell, P. W., Wilson, M. B., Lynch, H. K., Spitz, M. R., and Hersh, E. M. (1985). Risk factors analysis among men referred for possible acquired immune deficiency syndrome. *Preventive Medicine, 14,* 81–91.

Nurco, D., Wegner, N., and Stephanson, T. (1982). Female narcotic addicts changing profiles. *Journal of Addiction and Health, 62,* 105.

Nyanjom, D., Greaves, W., Delapenha, R., Barnes, S., Boynes, F., and Frederick, W. R. (1987, June). *Sexual behavior change among HIV seropositive individuals.* Paper presented to the Third International Conference on AIDS, Washington, DC.

Ostrow, D. (1990). *Behavioral Aspects of AIDS.* New York and London: Plenum Medical Book Company.

Ostrow, D. G., Michaels, S., and Albrecht, G. L. (1987). *Information and misinformation: The state of knowledge, attitudes and beliefs about AIDS in the Chicago metropolitan area general population.* Report of the Comprehensive AIDS Prevention Education Program (CAPEP), Chicago Department of Public Health.

Padian, N. S., Shiboski, S. C., and Jewell, N. P. (1991, September 25). Female-to-male transmission of human immunodeficiency virus. *Journal of the American Medical Association, 266* (12), 1664–1667.

Pepin, J., Plummer, F. A., Brunham, R. C., Cameron, D. W., and Ronald, A. R. (1989). The interaction of HIV infection and other sexually transmitted diseases: An opportunity for intervention. *AIDS, 3,* 3–9.

Perloff, L. S. (1983). Perceptions of vulnerability to victimization. *Journal of Social Issues, 39,* 41–61.

Perloff, L. S., and Fetzer, B. K. (1986). Self-other judgments and perceived vulnerability to victimization. *Journal of Personality and Social Psychology, 50,* 502–510.

Perrow, C., and Guillen, M. F. (1990). *The AIDS disaster: The failure of organizations in New York and the nation.* New Haven, CT: Yale University Press.

Peterman, T. A., Jaffe, H. W., Feorino, P. M., Getchell, J. P., Warfield, D. T., Haverkos, H. W., Stoneburner, R. L., and Curran, J. W. (1985). Transfusion-associated acquired immunodeficiency syndrome in the United States. *Journal of the American Medical Association, 254,* 2913–2919.

Pettigrew, A. H., and Pettigrew, T. F. (1974). Race, disease, and desegregation: A new look. In A. Shiloh and I. C. Selevan (Eds.), *Ethnic groups of America: Their morbidity, mortality and behavior disorders, Vol. 2*, (pp. 36–63). Springfield, IL: Thomas Books.

Pleck, J. H. (1989). Correlates of Black Adolescent Males' Condom Use. *Journal of Adolescent Research, 4* (2), 247–253.

Pleck, J. H., Stonenstein, F. L., and Swain, S. O. (1988). Adolescent males' sexual behavior and contraceptive use: Implications for male responsibility. *Journal of Adolescent Research, 3,* 275–284.

Polk, B. F., Fox, R., Brookmeyer, R., Kanchanaraka, S., Kaslow, R., Visscher, B., Rinaldo, C., and Phair, J. (1987). Predictors of the acquired immuno-deficiency syndrome developing in a cohort of seropositive homosexual men. *New England Journal of Medicine, 316,* 61–67.

Positive HTLV-III/LAV antibody results for sexually active female members of social/sexual clubs—Minnesota. (1987b). *Journal of the American Medical Association, 257,* 293–296.

Primm, B. J. (1990, February 9). *AIDS and intravenous drug use.* Paper presented at HIV in Sunbelt Conference at Texas Southern University in Houston.

Quinn, T. C. (1990). The epidemiology of the human immunodeficiency virus. *Annals of Emergency Medicine, 19,* 225–232.

Quinn, T. C., Cannon, R. O., Glasser, D., Groseclose, S. L., Brathwaite, W. S., Fauci, A. S., and Hook, E. W. (1990). The association of syphilis with risk of human immunodeficiency virus infection in patients attending sexually transmitted disease clinics. *Archives of Internal Medicine, 150,* 1297–1302.

Rabkin, C. S., Thomas, P. A., Jaffe, H. W., and Schultz, S. (1987). Prevalence of antibody to HTLV-III/LAV in a population attending a sexually trans-mitted disease clinic. *Sexually Transmitted Diseases, 14,* 48–51.

Rand, C. S. W., and Kuldau, J. M. (1990). The epidemiology of obesity and self-defined weight problem in the general population: Gender, race, age, and social class. *International Journal of Eating Disorders, 9,* 329–343.

Randolph, L. B. (1991, January). Thinking the unthinkable: Man-sharing. *Ebony,* 136–140.

Rapp, F. (1989). Sexually transmitted viruses. *The Yale Journal of Biology and Medicine, 62,* 173–185.

Redfield, R. R., Markman, P. D., Salahuddin, S. Z., Wright, D. C., Sarngadharan, M. G., and Gallo, R. C. (1987). Heterosexual acquired HTLV-III/LAV disease (AIDS-related complex and AIDS): Epidemiologic evidence for female-to-male transmission. *Journal of the American Medical Association, 254,* 2094–2096.

Reinisch, J. M., Sanders, S. A., and Zimba-Davis, M. (1988). The study of sexual behavior in relation to the transmission of human immunodeficiency virus. Caveats and recommendations. *American Psychologist, 43* (11), 921–927.

Rickert, V. I., Gottlieb, A., and Jay, S. M. (1990). A comparison of three clinic-based AIDS education programs on female adolescents' knowledge, attitudes, and behavior. *Journal of Adolescent Health Care, 11,* 298–303.

Rickert, V., Jay, S., Gottlieb, A., and Bridges, C. (1989). Female's attitudes and behavior toward condom purchase use. *Journal of Adolescent Health Care, 10,* 313–316.

Rietmeijer, C., Krebs, J. W., Feorino, P. M., and Judson, F. N. (1987, June). *In vitro tests demonstrate condoms containing nonoxynol-9 provide effective physical and chemical barriers against human immunodeficiency virus.* Paper presented to the Third International Conference on AIDS, Washington, DC.

Ripley, W. K. (1985). Medium of presentation: Does it make a difference in the reception of evaluation information. *Educ Eval Policy Analysis, 7,* 417–425.

Risk factors for AIDS among Haitians residing in the United States: Evidence of heterosexual transmission: The Collaborative Study Group of AIDS in Haitian-Americans. (1987a). *Journal of the American Medical Association, 257,* 635–639.

Rolfs, R. T., and Coates, W., Jr. (1989). The perpetual lessons of syphilis. *Arc Dermatology, 125,* 107–109.

Rolfs, R. T., Goldberg, M., and Alexander, E. R. (1988). Drug related behavior and syphilis in Philadelphia: "Sex for drugs" (abstract). *American Journal of Epidemiology, 128,* 898.

Rooney, J. F., Felser, J. M., Ostrove, J. M., and Straus, S. E. (1986). Acquisition of genital herpes from an asymptomatic sexual partner. *New England Journal of Medicine, 314,* 1561–1564.

Roscoe, B., and Kruger, T. L. (1990). AIDS: Late adolescents' knowledge and its influence on sexual behavior. *Adolescence, 25,* 39–48.

Rothenberg, R., Woelfel, M., Stoneburner, R., Milburg, J., Parker, R., and Truman, B. (1987). Survival with the Acquired Immunodeficiency Syndrome. *New England Journal of Medicine, 317,* 1297–1302.

Sandholzer, T. A. (1983). Factors affecting the incidence and management of sexually transmitted diseases in homosexual men. In D. G. Ostrow, T. A. Sandholzer, and Y. M. Feldman (Eds.), *Sexually Transmitted Diseases in Homosexual Men* (pp. 3–12). New York: Plenum Medical Book Company.

Saunders, J. (1989). Psychosocial and cultural issues in HIV infection. *Seminars in Oncology Nursing, 5,* 284–288.

Scesney, S. M., Gantz, N. M., and Sullivan, J. L. (1987, June). *Impermeability of condoms to HIV and inactivation of HIV by the spermicide nonoxynol-9.* Paper presented to the Third International Conference on AIDS, Washington, DC.

Schacter, J. (1989). Why we need a program to control Chlamydia trachomatis. *New England Journal of Medicine, 320,* 802–803.

Schultz, S., Friedman, S., and Kristal, A. (1984). Declining rates of rectal and pharyngeal gonorrhea among males—New York City. *Morbidity and Mortality Weekly Report, 33,* 295–297.

Schwarcz, S. K., and Rutherford, G. W. (1989). Acquired immunodeficiency syndrome in infants, children, and adolescents. *Journal of Drug Issues, 19,* 75–92.

Scott, J. (1976, Summer). Polygamy: A Futuristic Family Arrangement for

African-Americans. *Black Books Bulletin.*

Seale, J. (1985). AIDS virus infection: Prognosis and transmission. *Journal of the Royal Society of Medicine, 78,* 613–615.

Seltzer, R., and Smith, R. C. (1988). Racial differences and intra-racial differences among blacks in attitudes toward AIDS. *Child and Youth Services, 9,* 31–35.

Seltzer, R., Gilliam, A., and Stroman, C. (1988). *Public perceptions of AIDS in the District of Columbia: Knowledge and attitudes.* Washington, DC: Institute for Urban Affairs and Research, Howard University Press.

Shilts, R. (1988). *And the band played on: Politics, people, and the AIDS epidemic.* New York: Penguin Books.

Siegel, K., Mesagno, F., Chen, J. Y., and Christ, G. (1987, June). *Factors distinguishing homosexual males practicing safe and risky sex.* Paper presented to the Third International Conference on AIDS, Washington, DC.

Spielberger, C. D. (1988). *Professional Manual for the State-Trait Anger Expression Inventory (STAXI)* (Research ed.). Tampa, FL: Psychological Assessment Resources.

Spielberger, C. D., Jacobs, G., Russell, S., and Crane, R. (1983). Assessment of anger: The state-trait anger scale. In J. N. Butcher and C. D. Spielberger (Eds.), *Advances in personality assessment* (Vol. 2). Hillsdale, NJ: Lawrence Erlbaum and Associates.

Stall, R., McKusick, L., Wiley, J., Coates, T., and Ostrow, D. (1986). Alcohol and drug use during sexual activity and compliance with safe sex guidelines for AIDS: The AIDS behavioral research project. *Health Education Quarterly, 13,* 359–371.

Stevens, C. E., Taylor, P. E., Zang, E. A., Rodriguez de Cordoba, S., and Rubinstein, P. (1987, June). *Incidence of HIV infection in homosexual men in a high risk area: Implications for vaccine trial design.* Paper presented to the Third International Conference on AIDS, Washington, DC.

Strunin, L., and Hingson, R. (1987). Acquired immunodeficiency syndrome and adolescents: Knowledge, beliefs, attitudes, and behaviors. *Pediatrics, 79,* 825–828.

Tanner, W. M., and Pollack, R. H. (1988). The effect of condom use and erotic instructions on attitudes toward condoms. *The Journal of Sex Research, 25,* 537–541.

Tavris, C. (1982). *Anger: The Misunderstood Emotion.* New York: Simon and Schuster.

Tavris, C., and Sands, S. (1975). *The Redbook Report on Female Sexuality.* New York: Delacourte.

Thomas, S. B., Gilliam, A. G., and Iwrey, C. G. (1989). Knowledge about AIDS and reported risk behaviors among black college students. *Journal of American College Health, 38,* 8–13.

Thompson, S. E., and Washington, A. E. (1983). Epidemiology of sexually transmitted chlamydia trachomatis infections. *Epidemiology Reviews, 5,* 96–123.

Thurman, Q. C., and Franklin, K. M. (1990). AIDS and college health: Knowledge, threat, and prevention at a northeastern university. *Journal of American College Health, 38,* 179–183.

Turner, C. F., Miller, H. G., and Moses, L. E. (1989). *AIDS: Sexual Behavior and Intravenous Drug Use.* Washington, DC: National Research Council, National Academy Press.

Turner, C., Anderson, P., Fitzpatrick, R., Fowler, G., and Mayon-White, R. (1988). Sexual behavior, contraceptive practice and knowledge of AIDS of Oxford University students. *Journal of Biosocial Science, 20,* 445–451.

U.S. Department of Health and Human Services. (1985, August). Report of the Secretary's Task Force on Black and Minority Health. Washington, DC.

Upchurch, D. M, Farmer, M. Y., Glasser, D., and Hook, E. W. (1987). Contraceptive needs and practices among women attending an inner-city STD clinic. *American Journal of Public Health, 77,* 1427–1430.

Vacalis, T. D., Shoemaker, P. J., and McAlister, A. (1989). A baseline study of AIDS in Texas: Knowledge, attitudes, and behaviors. *Texas Medicine, 85,* 74–79.

Valdiserri, R., Lyter, D., Leviton, L. C., Callahan, C. M., Kingsley, L. A., and Rinaldo, C. R. (1988). Variables influencing condom use in a cohort of gay and bisexual men. *American Journal of Public Health, 78,* 801–805.

Van de Perre, P., Jacobs, D., and Sprecher-Goldberger, S. (1987). The latex condom, an efficient barrier against sexual transmission of AIDS-related viruses. *AIDS, 1,* 49–52.

Van de Perre, P., Rouvroy, D., Lepage, P., Bogaerts, J., Kestelyn, P., Kayihigi, J., Hekker, A. C., Butzler, J. P., and Clumeck, N. (1984). Acquired immunodeficiency syndrome in Rwanda. *Lancet, 2,* 62–65.

Vonderheide, S. G., and Mosher, D. L. (1988). Should I put in my diaphragm? Sex-guilt and turn-offs. *Journal of Psychology and Human Sexuality, 1,* 97–111.

Washington, A. E., Johnson, R. E., Sanders, L. L., Barnes, R. C., and Alexander, E. R. (1986). Incidence of chlamydia trachomatis infections in the United States: Using reported Neisseria gonorrhoeae as a surrogate. In D. Oriel, G. Ridgway, J. Schachter, D. Taylor-Robinson, and M. Ward (Eds.), *Chlamydial Infections* (p. 487). Cambridge, England: Cambridge University Press.

Weber, J. N., Wadsworth, J., Rogers, L. A., Moshitael, O., Scott, K., McManus, T., Berrie, E., Jefferies, D. J., Harris, J. R., and Pinching, A. J. (1986). Three-year prospective study of HTLV-III/LAV infection in homosexual men. *Lancet, 1,* 1179–1182.

Weinstein, M., Goodjoin, R. B., Crayton, E. C., and Lawson, C. M. (Eds.). (1988). Black sexuality: A bibliography (2nd ed.). San Francisco: University of California.

Weinstein, N. D. (1980). Unrealistic optimism about future life events. *Journal of Personality and Social Psychology, 39,* 806–820.

Whittington, W. L., and Knapp, J. S. (1988). Trends in resistance Neisseria gonorrhoeae to antimicrobial agents in the United States. *Sexually Transmitted Diseases, 15,* 202–210.

Williams, D. C. (1979). Sexually transmitted diseases in gay men: An insider's view (editorial). *Sexually Transmitted Diseases, 6* (4), 278–280.

Williams, R. B. (1989). *The Trusting Heart.* New York: Times Books, Random House.

Willoughby, B., Schechter, M. T., Boyko, W. J., Craib, K. J. P., Weaver, M. S., and Douglas, B. (1987, June). *Sexual practices and condom use in a cohort of homosexual men. Evidence of differential modification between seropositive and seronegative men.* Paper presented to the Third International Conference on AIDS, Washington, DC.

Winkelstein, W., Jr., Lyman, D., Padin, G., Grant, R., Samuel, M., Wiley, J., Anderson, R., Lang, W., Riggs, J., and Levy, J. (1987). Sexual practices and risk of infection by the HIV virus: The San Francisco Men's Health Study. *Journal of the American Medical Association, 257,* 321–325.

Winslow, R. W. (1988). Student knowledge of AIDS transmission. *Sociology and Social Research, 72,* 110–113.

Wolcott, D. L. (1986a). Psychosocial aspects of acquired immune deficiency syndrome and the primary care physician. *Annals of Allergy, 57,* 98–102.

——. (1986b). Neuropsychiatric syndromes in AIDS and AIDS-related diseases. In L. McKusick (Ed.), *What to do about AIDS: Physicians and mental health professionals discuss the issues* (pp. 46–62). Berkeley: University of California Press.

Worth, D. M., and Rodriguez, R. (1987). Latino women and AIDS. *Radical America, 21,* 63–67.

Zabin, L. S., Hardy, J. B., Smith, E. A., and Hirsch, M. B. (1986). Substance use and its relation to sexual activity among inner-city adolescents. *Journal of Adolescent Health Care, 7,* 320–331.

Index

ABOUT THE AUTHOR

ERNEST H. JOHNSON is Associate Professor of Family Medicine and Director of Behavioral Medicine Research at Morehouse School of Medicine in Atlanta. He is the founder and editor-in-chief of *Ethnic Perspectives on Health and Behavior,* a Praeger series. Dr. Johnson is the author of *The Deadly Emotions: Anger, Hostility, and Aggression in Health and Emotional Well-Being* (Praeger, 1990) and a co-editor of *Personality, Elevated Blood Pressure, and Essential Hypertension* (1990). Recently he started *Body and Spirit — The African-American's Guide to Optimal Health,* a quarterly health news journal for the general public. Dr. Johnson has published various articles in professional journals and books on the health problems of African-Americans.